T0072549

RAISING
KANYE

RAISING KANYE

Life Lessons from the
Mother of a Hip-Hop Superstar

Donda West

with Karen Hunter

POCKET BOOKS

NEW YORK   LONDON   TORONTO   SYDNEY

Pocket Books
A Division of Simon & Schuster, Inc.
1230 Avenue of the Americas
New York, NY 10020

First Pocket Books hardcover edition May 2007

POCKET and colophon are registered trademarks
of Simon & Schuster, Inc.

For information about special discounts for bulk purchases,
please contact Simon & Schuster Special Sales at
1-800-456-6798 or business@simonandschuster.com

Designed by Mary Austin Speaker

Manufactured in the United States of America

10 9 8 7 6 5 4 3 2 1

ISBN-13: 978-1-4165-4478-4
ISBN-10:   1-4165-4478-X

Dedicated to the memory of my sister, Klaye Jones,
whose laughter was a smile set to music.

I'll hear her laughter forever.

Acknowledgments

I am deeply grateful to my mother and father for making me who I am, and to Kanye West for being my greatest joy.

To my entire family for always believing in me. To Miki Woodard, Jeanella Blair, Bill Johnson, Sakiya Sandifer, Alexis Phifer, Michael Newton, Damien Dziepak, Stephan Scoggins, and to my editor, Lauren McKenna for invaluable feedback on the manuscript.

To Adlaidie Walker and Terry Horton for encouraging me to be bold. To the James Hotel in Chicago for incredible hospitality while I worked there on the manuscript. To Ann and Ralph Hines for providing me with the perfect place to retreat and for being the perfect hosts.

To Jahon Rashid, Linda Ames, and Sonya Spencer for rescuing me from a writing marathon and encouraging me to return to it. To Ian Kleinert for selling Simon & Schuster on the vision, to Simon & Schuster for seeing the vision and providing this opportunity.

To Lou Takacs, Brad Rose, Robert Stein, and Alison Finley for outstanding legal counsel. To Jennifer Rudolph Walsh for scrutinizing this deal. To Sheila Roberson and Janelle Keith for critical research and follow up. To Reshawn Jackson for being the perfect model, to Jean Roberson for supplying the model. To Tre Major (cover photo hair and makeup) for attentiveness to every detail and incredible workmanship. To Charlene Roxbury (wardrobe), to Sharron Winbush for nutrition and physical training throughout this process. To Jon Platt at EMI Publishing. To Gabe Tesoriero, Al Branch, and Jeanella Blair for promoting the book.

To Gee Roberson, Shawn Gee, Susan Linns, Sheila Roberson, John Monopoly, Ibn Jasper, Don Crawley, Alison Finley, Brett Goetsch, Barry Ray, Al Branch, and John Hicks for always having Kanye's back (and mine, too). To Stephan Scoggins for always inspiring me.

And to Karen Hunter for being a brilliant cowriter without whom I could never have done this project.

Foreword

by Kanye West

I've known my mom since I was zero years old. She is quite dope. What stands out most about her is not only how she taught me but her willingness to learn new things and that she listens to me.

When some people become parents, they are so busy teaching, they sometimes close off to learning. A lot of parents are so stuck in their ways they can't adjust to new things. You have to be in touch with what your kids are doing. You have to be a part of them.

If parents could be more open-minded to their children, more open to what their children are into—like their music, their clothes, and their interests—maybe they could raise children who become open-minded adults. That's how my mom was. And I was open to what she told me because she always valued what I had to say.

I remember one time we were having a discussion about

proper English. I was saying something and asked her if it was proper. She told me it depends. Language is situational.

"If you're in a room full of people and everyone is speaking Ebonics and you break out with the Queen's English, super proper, then even if you're speaking so-called correct English, you're not correct. To communicate effectively, you have to speak so that people can understand you."

I remembered that when I wrote my songs. And she in turn lived it. It was nothing for her to break out into perfect Ebonics. "What up, dog?"

When I wrote that song, "Hey...Mama!" about my mom, I worked on it for months. I wanted to make it as great as she is. I wanted to tell the whole world about our friendship and how it came to be. I also wanted to talk about her in the most artistic way I could. I wanted her to know how much I appreciate her for the way she raised me.

You'll see that in these pages and you'll learn things that I didn't even know until I read this book. But what I did know is that because of who she is, I am able to be who I am.

Contents

Raising Kanye

He was about seven months old when I first noticed it. Actually, I didn't notice it; someone else
pointed it out to me. Kanye was sitting in his
stroller in a vegetarian restaurant in Atlanta with
his middle and index fingers in his mouth (he sucked
those two fingers until he was eight). This lady
came into the restaurant and stopped in her
tracks.

"Look at that face!" she said.

I looked and she was staring at Kanye, almost mesmerized. I thought to myself, "Yes, he
is cute, isn't he?" But then he looked up at me and
I saw it, too. I saw what she was talking about. He looked at
me with eyes that spoke. And I knew, like the old folks sometimes know when they see certain babies, "He was an old
soul."

While he was still in my womb, I used to pray for my child. Everyone prays for their child to be healthy—to have all their fingers and toes. I prayed that prayer, but I added to it brilliance. I prayed for my child to be healthy *and* brilliant. That day in the restaurant, I knew my prayers had been answered—beyond my wildest imagination. I never imagined that I would be the mother of someone quite as unique as Kanye West, someone God had chosen to do something very special in the world.

Looking back, I've thought many times about what makes Kanye Kanye. Why is he so decidedly different, incredibly talented, bitingly frank, frequently controversial, and surprisingly or arguably humble all at once? Undoubtedly, who Kanye is today has a great deal to do with the way he was brought up, his exposure to the world, his relationship with his parents, the impact of his grandparents, the "you go, boy" of friends and family, the hard work of his team, the drive within him, and most of all, the goodness of God.

This book is a journey into who he is. But it is also my story, my journey as a mother—at times a single mother—just trying to raise a healthy and productive child. And somewhere along the way, the journey led to greatness.

It's said that at some point you become your parents. I believe that your parents have a tremendous impact on the kind of parent you become. My father, Portwood Williams Sr., and my mother, Lucille Williams, influenced my parenting tremendously. They loved and supported me. Never did I want for anything, materially or otherwise. It wasn't that we were well off. In fact, mother always said we were poor. But I never felt poor. In fact, I felt just the opposite. My sisters and brother and I were made to feel rich.

We had material things because my parents were very resourceful. But more importantly, our lives were filled with love, adoration, and congratulations. Kids pay attention to what they don't have monetarily only when there is a real lack of everything else. In my home, my parents made us all feel that nothing came before us, except God. I was the same with Kanye. He knew how highly I thought of him.

He also knew I had high expectations of him. A lot of people like to coddle their children. They don't want to hurt their feelings, or make them feel bad for not achieving. But if you don't set benchmarks, and if you don't set that bar high, you can't expect your children to excel. My parents required every one of us not just to do our best, but to be *the* best. They didn't demand it in an overbearing, make-you-want-to-jump-out-of-the-window-if-you-don't-get-an-A sort of way. It was just quietly but assuredly expected.

Once, in seventh grade, I brought home five As and a B. My dad looked at me and said, "That's good, Big Girl [I was the baby of four and that was my nickname]. But why did you make the B?"

It was a good question. I had made the B in home economics. I was never big on cooking, sewing, knitting, and all the other rather mundane (or so I thought) tasks we were required to perform in Mrs. Ricks's class. I got a B because I didn't do my best and my father knew it. My father gave me five dollars—he would give me a dollar for every A. I didn't really care about the money as much as the praise. But this time I felt shortchanged—I had shortchanged myself because I didn't do my very best. That simple question—"But why did you make a B?"—was all I needed to not want to make a B again.

My father always had a way of making me feel that I was

the most special and the smartest person on earth, and I never wanted to disappoint him. I'm told that when I was born he said, "I'll make her a masterpiece." I have absorbed those words into my being—in my mind, spirit, and actions. I prayed that prayer to make my child brilliant, in the same vein as my father wanting to make me a masterpiece.

I am grateful to have had a road map, a blueprint to parent, laid down by my mother and father. There was no need for me to reinvent the wheel. Emulating great parents is just common sense. It's a way of keeping or returning to some of those old-fashioned values. Now, I didn't follow them to the letter. Sometimes, if paradigm shifts were needed, I chose not to emulate them. But there was one constant: I made sure that Kanye always knew he was loved—not just doted on and indulged, but loved. That is the only advice my father ever verbally gave me about raising Kanye. And I never forgot it.

When I watch Kanye today, I see in him the courage of my dad and the strength of my mother, the diligence of his father's dad and the devotedness of his father's mother. I see the creativity of his dad, Ray West, and my sensitivity. Kanye embodies aspects of the entire West and Williams families. Sometimes impatient, he is also able to endure what many cannot. I see in him the passion of Christ, but not always the patience of Job.

Just as I am my parents' child, Kanye is very much his parents' child. Like his dad, Kanye has little patience for what he thinks is unjust. If he sees a president leave human beings stranded on rooftops for days at a time, his passion and compassion will outweigh his patience. And the media is likely to witness what it calls outrageous outbursts. What is actually outrageous is the situation prompting the "outburst." His fiery statements never anger or embarrass me. I know they come from not only the situation at hand but also his legacy.

As much as I have tried to give to Kanye, I believe in many ways I have gotten so much more from him. While this book is about raising Kanye, in many ways, Kanye has raised me. He has taught me so much. One of the most valuable lessons I learned from him was to always tell the truth. I have learned many other lessons from him, as well, which I will share within these pages. But telling the truth at all costs is not always easy to do. We live in a society where everyone wants to put on a good face, wants to look good no matter what. But the truth sometimes is very ugly and you have to stand strong in those times when the ugly truth has to be told—when you have to come face-to-face with your own ugliness or the ugliness of those who might persecute you for telling the truth. I appreciate Kanye for being truthful.

I really do believe that our children are not *our* children—they are souls that come through us to fulfill their purpose. We are here largely to give life to them so that they might give life, figuratively or physically, to others. I believe that we must listen to our children so that we may teach them well the lessons that God would have them learn. In fact, listening is the only way we can be effective in our teaching.

Strong and effective parenting requires that we give more than lip service to the phrase "out of the mouths of babes." As we train them, they teach us—if we're open to it.

I believe children come here with wisdom. They have gifts that are uniquely theirs. And because they are still children, they are not yet constrained the way adults often are. That's why, for example, they pick up languages easier than adults do. Kanye and I spent a year in China. While I struggled to put together simple phrases, before we left, he was able to speak and understand the language fairly well.

Children don't have all of the barriers we have. They aren't steeped in tradition and bogged down by rules that tell them what they cannot do or how things must be done. The best thing a parent can do for a child is to not teach them the wrong kinds of traditions, those that foster fear and insecurities.

Another lesson I got from Kanye was tolerance. Actually, that was something that we taught each other. Often, we teach best what we most need to learn and we get the lesson back in the reflection of our children. They become our mirror to see the things we really need to work on, and Kanye was that mirror for me.

He taught me to reserve judgment by calling me out every time I was judgmental. And he did so simply by throwing my own words right back at me. He also taught me patience and how to put things into a proper or the best perspective.

One time, we were rushing to the airport so he could catch a plane to visit his dad, as he did every summer. Kanye insisted that we take a certain route to miss the traffic. We missed the traffic but were stopped by a long freight train. I was next to furious because I'd purchased one of those bargain-rate tickets for which there was no refund if you didn't use it. And I didn't have that kind of money to waste, nor did I really have it to buy another ticket. I grew frustrated as I contemplated all of that and I started ranting and raving about how we should have just taken the regular route and how he was going to miss the plane. Kanye just looked at me. And out of his twelve-year-old mouth came, "Mom, only something that will help. Only something that will help."

The words hit me as hard as that freight train would have had we kept driving not to miss that plane. I was actually stunned. It wasn't about getting the pressure off him as much as it was about making me think. It was about me engaging in conversation that would be helpful—not ranting and raving uselessly. No bringing energy to the situation that could only exacerbate it. "Only something that will help."

To this day, I try to live by those words.

We ended up making it to the airport just in time. Kanye did catch his plane and we didn't have to buy another ticket.

Now, don't get me wrong, it wasn't all peaches and honey raising my son. There were many challenges. But the challenges were actually opportunities to learn and grow. They were just part of life.

I became a single mother early in Kanye's life. His dad and I had been happily married for nearly four years by the time Kanye came along. But we separated when Kanye was just eleven months old and divorced when he was three. Some serious differences of opinion surfaced that were seemingly insurmountable. I joined the ranks of the majority of black mothers in this country—more than seventy percent of black children are born to single mothers.

My story is very much like theirs in some ways, but in other ways very different. We lived in cities—Atlanta and Chicago—where we had no immediate family. There was no grandmother or auntie to drop Kanye off with, no built-in babysitter to provide the comfort of knowing my child would be safe. There was no one there to pick us up and drop me off at work and Kanye at day care when the car broke down— which happened a lot in those days. There was no dollar or two slipped in my pocket for those little extras or even the necessities. It was just Kanye and me. And I had to make it happen.

One of the biggest challenges for me early on was how to discipline Kanye without killing his spirit—how to support who he was and at the same time give him boundaries that would keep him within the parameters of what is appropriate. You may laugh and ask, "Kanye, appropriate?" And to that I would reply, "Yes, appropriate." To me, being appropriate does not always mean conforming. Often it means just the opposite. Sometimes, refusing to conform and even confronting is not only appropriate but necessary to change the world for the better. It was not always an easy thing to draw the line between what warranted polite behavior and agreement and what did not.

I always wanted Kanye to be polite. But I was not of the mind set that anything any adult did was correct and that the child was always wrong. I believe that adults must always be respected, if not for their right actions or thoughts, certainly for their age. But I was determined not to send mixed messages to Kanye.

It was my job as a parent to figure it out. When do I shout (if ever), and when do I calmly explain the situation and welcome feedback in the same calm tone? I concluded that 99.9 percent of the time, the latter was more effective. I was lucky. I had a son who I could reason with from a very early age. He was not a timid and passive child by any means. And on more than a few occasions I had to struggle just to control *my* temper. I had to calm down before I could reason with him.

Another challenge was how to provide for him without totally spoiling him. I had to balance the extent to which I would allow him to have things and when I would tell him no. Rarely did I tell Kanye no. I gave him most everything he asked for—at least what I could afford. I would figure out a way to borrow from Peter to pay Paul so that ultimately, he could have it. Why? Because Kanye earned it. He had to. I didn't just hand things over without requiring that he do his part—whether it was making good grades or doing his chores. And he was a good kid. Had he not been, things would have been different. Had he talked back to me and refused to do what I asked of him, I would not have rewarded him. To do so would have been to enable a brat, not raise a child. And that, more than anything, would have been a disservice to *him*.

There was an occasion or two when I had to put Kanye in his place. I don't believe in children raising their voices to their parents. It simply was not acceptable. It was not an option, and Kanye always knew that. So when he tried it once or twice, I had to shut that down.

I'm grateful that I was able to give Kanye most everything he wanted. But I am thankful that I realized the importance of establishing the groundwork. Giving kids whatever they want without first giving them everything they need—a solid foundation of morals, expectations, and discipline—is not parenting. It's irresponsible and wrong. You're not showing love just because you give your child anything he or she wants. That's letting a kid grow up like a weed while you're just standing by watching and watering.

I cannot take total credit for the man Kanye turned out to be. It does take a village. I couldn't have done it alone. There are many women who are single parents—but being a single mom doesn't mean you have to raise your children alone. That's my belief. Single mothers with sons are obliged to find strong, positive male figures who can be a model to their sons.

Kanye had a father and I made sure he spent his summers with him. He had two grandfathers, who he saw as often as possible. He had uncles who he got to know and learn from. And there were my male friends who were there to lend a hand. I was very fortunate. There were several men in my life Kanye could learn from, exchange ideas, and share his thoughts with, and from whom he could learn how to be a man.

Now, there is a flip side to this. As a single mother, you have to be very careful about not exposing your children to too many men. Having a revolving door of "uncles" and your love interests sends the wrong message. I am a red-blooded woman with needs that I didn't sacrifice just because I had a child. But I just picked my spots. I didn't have a parade of men coming through. I had to be sure about the relationship (and it had to be a relationship, not just some fling) before I had a man meet my son. I used his summers with his father to see what was what—that's when I did most of my dating and feeling out.

One of the men who stuck around was Scotty. He taught auto mechanics at what is now Simeon Career Academy in Chicago. I met him when Kanye was ten. A year later we were engaged and living together. Although we never married, Kanye has told me more than once that Scotty is one of the reasons he is a responsible man today. Scotty was a stern man who had high standards and wouldn't let Kanye get away with anything. With me, Kanye would moan and groan about putting out the trash or doing other chores. When Scotty said do it, he did it without a word.

Scotty wasn't a big man in size. He was short and stocky with a deep voice; but he was a strong man with good character. There is a certain language, spoken or unspoken, between males. There is an understanding, a toughness, a demeanor that signals to boys that they cannot cross the lines with a man that they may cross with their mothers.

I was demanding, but in some ways still typical of many mothers. If Kanye forgot to take out the garbage, I would run to take it out, fussing all the while with a "what am I going to do with that boy" attitude. Kanye knew that Scotty wasn't having it. If Scotty said put out the garbage, there was no forgetting.

There are many men who have grown up to be strong, successful, and wise without the influence of a strong man in their lives—my father being a prime example. But those men are anomalies, the exception, not the rule.

I've heard some women say they don't need a man. And perhaps for them that is true. But if they have children, I beg to differ.

Children, whether boys or girls, need men in their lives. This is particularly true of boys. If you don't believe it, ask all of the men who are currently in our prison system. More than ninety percent of them grew up without a father or father figure. It's not just a male that is needed, however. It's a man—one who will take the time to talk with your child, who has something useful to add to the equation.

I believe that men are equally important in the raising of a girl, too. I can't imagine what my life would have been like and who I would have become had I not had my dad with me. Sometimes people do grow up and become okay people, even great people. But I'd bet ninety-five percent of the people raised without a man in their lives have some issues that they wish they didn't. Maybe they have issues they can't even identify, largely due to the absence of that father figure.

From his dad (the creative intellectual), to my brother (the music virtuoso), to my father (the thinker and provider), to Scotty (the no-nonsense general), to a small host of good men, both family and friends, Kanye was exposed to real men, which was key in his becoming a man. He was able to flex his manhood in ways he never would have without their input.

When I was approached to do a book about my experiences raising Kanye West, I had never imagined actually writing a book about that. But now it makes perfect sense.

I had fancied writing a book one day. But I thought it might be about my different dating experiences. I had lots of little clever titles, like "The Jaded Janitor" and "The Crazy Cop." I was going to share those life experiences and hopefully come full circle to finding my ultimate soul mate.

But the man I ended up writing about is the man who, to date, has had perhaps the most profound impact on my life: my son. And what makes this project extra special to me is that I get to share what he has meant not only to me but also to music and to a generation.

A lot of people think Kanye turned out really well. He's such a departure from what people see as a typical rapper. With his life being so exposed to the world—at least the part that is exposed—there is still so much to share, so many questions to answer.

When I was little, I used to travel and compete in oratorical contests with my church. We would compete against other churches from across the country. I would have to act out Bible passages or give speeches about a particular scrip-

ture. My dad always encouraged me. Before we'd leave for
one of those many competitions, Daddy would turn to me and
say, "Big Girl, you have to have a story for the people. You
got your story?"

I have my story: *Raising Kanye*.

1

Back to the Future

How many folks do you know
Who can boast about their dad?
And say that he's the best there is
The best they could have had?

How many folks can tell you
That their dad is really hip?
Our kind of conversation
Might cause some folks to trip.

Well here is one who'll talk of you
Until this life is through
And when I get to someplace else
I'll still be talking about you.

—DONDA WEST, "A Man Called Portwood"

The last time my daddy saw his own father, he was nine years old. He and his two sisters walked their father to the train station in Oklahoma City, where he boarded a train to a destination they would never know. My dad didn't remember any of the conversation. But he did remember his father reaching into his pocket and giving his older sister a dime, his younger sister a dime, and him—the only boy—a quarter. His father then turned and walked onto that train and never came back.

My father talks about how he and his sisters were very happy about the money, but inside they were sad to see their dad leave. My father's mother had not gone to the train station. When she learned about the little excursion, her eyes filled with tears. Maybe she knew that day would be the last time any of them would see him. All he left them with was a total of forty-five cents. Forty-five cents for the kids and tears for his wife.

But still, my dad loved his father dearly. Later, my father asked his mother if she'd loved him, too.

"I worshipped the ground he walked on," Grandmother Williams told him.

There were two lessons my father took away that day that he in turn passed along to his children. The first was that no matter what, you never abandon your family. The second was that no matter what, you must love unconditionally. That his mother still loved his father—in fact, worshipped the ground he walked on—even after he walked out on the family showed a kind of love that you just don't find every day. They say you must hate the sin but love the sinner. You can hate what someone does and still love the person.

It is that kind of love that made my father the kind of father, and the kind of man, he is. My daddy vowed that he would never leave—he would never walk away from his family. And he never did. It's been seventy-two years of marriage . . . and counting—four kids, grandkids, great-grandkids, great-great-grandkids later—and he's still here. He and my mother laid the foundation for the rest of us to build upon and grow on.

> You took me with you everyplace
> From church to corner joints
> I learned when I was 5 or less
> About life's finer points.
>
> And when I wouldn't talk up
> The way you knew I should
> You gave me words of warning
> And then I knew I could.
>
> "I won't take you with me, Big Girl,
> If you don't speak out loud."
> And ever since I've talked right out
> To a few or in a crowd.
>
> When anything was needed
> You told me what to do
> "You have not, 'cause you ask not."
> Those words stuck with me too.

I remember everything my father ever told me. He never understood what would make a man leave his family. I know times were tough when my daddy was a child, so tough that he picked cotton. When he got older he worked for years on jobs where he was called "nigger" on a daily basis. And when he wasn't being called "nigger," the word of choice was "boy." Long before he rose to the honor of being one of Oklahoma

City's Outstanding Black Businessmen, my dad shined shoes and grinned for tips.

"Yes, sir," he'd say to the white men, who on occasion would even spit on him. Then he'd put that dime in his pocket and bring it home to my mom. My dad knew how to take the insults and keep his dignity. It must have eaten him alive inside but no one would ever know. Sometimes he had to flee for his very life. That's the way it was in those days. And if you wanted to provide the best you could for your family, you took it because you had to.

In Capitol Hill, a southern section of Oklahoma City where my dad worked as a laborer, there was a sign that read: NO NIGGERS AND DOGS AFTER SUNDOWN. My dad had to pass that sign every day going to and coming from his meager job. But he did whatever it took to keep a roof over our heads and, with my mother's help, give us what we needed and wanted.

Some would say it was blasphemous the way Grandmother Williams worshipped her husband, the way my dad worshipped me, and the way I worship Kanye. But I just call it plain-old heartfelt, couldn't-help-it-if-you-tried-to love. In my family there is a legacy of that kind of love. And there was no shortage of that in our household. It has persisted through generations. And I am certain that Kanye will feel the same way about his children.

My dad was just nine years old when his father left home. But instead of doing the same, Daddy became the kind of father his dad was not. I heard him say on more than one occasion, "I wanted to play football, but I wasn't big enough. I wanted to box, but I wasn't fast enough. I wanted to sing, but I wasn't talented enough. I wanted to be the best dad there ever was, and I am."

And he is—unequivocally.

According to Kanye, my dad is where he gets his confidence. My dad is in his nineties and he's still setting the standard in our family of what a real man, a daddy, not just a biological father, should be. I write about this because I look forward to Kanye becoming a father. He is blessed to have Buddy as a model.

A million days have come and come
Since I was first in school
But never did the teachers teach
What I have learned from you.

I got those books for you had said
That they could bring me glory
But more than that you taught me that
I'd have to have a story.

A story for the people
You'd say and show concern
That's been the greatest lesson
That I have ever learned.

You taught me how to hustle
And when to dummy up
Whatever the occasion
You had the proper touch.

The time that tops them all off, though
Was not so long ago

When we rapped and rode for hours
Down the streets there in Chicago.

That night the conversation
Seemed to linger in the air
And we both know without a doubt
We were a special pair.

So, I couldn't be more lucky
Than to have a dad like you
'Cause you're a priceless present
That I've had my whole life through.

You're a man that some call Portwood
And they say it with a smile
But I'm more blessed by far than they
'Cause I was born your child.

Love,
Big Girl

Behind every great man...you know the rest. With all that my father is, he is magnified by my mother. Unconditional love? Mother personified this. Not a single day passed in my childhood when anything came before her children. Not even her own needs. She was always wherever we needed her to be despite working full time. She didn't miss one PTA meeting, not one talent show or beauty pageant, not a church program or graduation. Mother didn't even miss a single graduation of her ten grandchildren. Sometimes she'd travel as far as El Paso, Texas, or Chicago, Illinois, to be there. She and my dad would be on a plane to that graduation.

Mine was the mother who took off work to go on field trips and the mother who made all the other kids glad she had come. As the youngest of the four children, I confess that I was in an enviable position. I got the fewest spankings and the best perks. We spent a lot of time together, mother and I. When she wasn't working at the Tinker Air Force Base or when I wasn't with my dad on a call to one of his customers (those demeaning jobs had now been replaced with my dad's own furniture upholstery and refinishing business), I hung out with Mother.

Every Monday night she would take me shopping downtown. Both of my sisters were grown and out of the house by then and my brother, Porty, would be in the shop mostly with my dad. Mother and I would hit John A. Brown's first and then Rothschild's. It was our routine. I didn't mind that we'd always go to the bargain basement first (and sometimes last). I loved it. I loved the time we spent together even more than the bargains she'd manage to always find for me. Mother is probably the one who came up with the concept "buy one, get one free." You could say that she could stretch a penny. A penny went far, but not nearly as far as her love.

Mother had not always worked as a keypunch operator at Tinker Air Force Base. I heard tell of stories where she'd done hair and been a domestic. My dad wanted her to stop doing hair, though, because she was on her feet too long. The domestic job? That bit the dust the day my mother went to work and rang the doorbell, as she had done so many mornings before to start her work, only to be met by the lady of the house, who I'll call Miss Ann. Miss Ann had come into some money and had a maid's outfit, complete with a little hat, ready for my mother.

"Use the back door from now on," she told my mother.

Well, you'd have to know my mother to know what this triggered inside of her. After giving the woman a few choice words, she left that house never to return. She was never to do domestic work again, either. She was not forced to take the same level of mistreatment my dad had to take. In fact, he would not stand for her being mistreated on a job. I don't remember hearing what my mother's next job was. But neither she nor my dad were okay with her being told to put on a little maid's hat and only use the back door. While my mother's mom was herself a domestic, Grandmother Eckles had never been treated like that. She worked for the Robinsons for forty-eight years and never suffered an unkind word from that family. In later years, they even sent for my grandmother by cab daily just to be a companion to Mrs. Robinson. They had hired another maid and cook by then and Grandmother's job was to keep Mrs. Robinson company. The Robinsons even paid off Grandmother Eckles's mortgage. I learned later that it was only a few thousand dollars, but paying the balance of the mortgage, no matter how small an amount, was a far cry from being told to put on a maid's hat and come in through the back door.

My mother couldn't and didn't take insults very well. When we went on our shopping sprees at John A. Brown, mother insisted that we use the "White Women" restroom and that we drink from the "Whites Only" water fountain. She must have had a presence that said to people, "Don't mess with me!" because rarely did anyone say anything to us. They just looked as if we ought to know better. What Mother knew is that my dad, as he'd often say, had picked enough cotton for us all. He'd picked cotton until his fingers bled. And he did it so that ultimately, his wife and his children would not have to, literally or figuratively.

Mother was always assertive, I'm told, even before she met my dad. Whether Kanye realizes it or not, he gets a lot of his fighting spirit and confidence from my mother, too.

Much of Kanye's confidence can also be traced from the West side. Mom-Mom was his paternal grandmother, Fannie B. Hooks West. Born in Arkansas, she met her husband, James Frederick West, in Tucson, Arizona, where Kanye's dad was born. After several months of courting, Mom-Mom demanded that James put up or shut up. She was not going to be the girlfriend, she was going to be the wife. After a relatively short courtship, Fannie and James married. James was a military man and remained so for twenty-three years. He, like my dad, was a protector and a provider. Unlike my dad, however, he lived in many places. The family traveled from Tucson, Arizona, to Salina, Kansas, to Delmar, Delaware, to Roswell, New Mexico, to Seville, Spain, to Altus, Oklahoma, back to Roswell, then to Marysville/Yuba City, California, and finally back to Delmar, where James, who Kanye called Pop-Pop, was born. Mom-Mom and Pop-Pop would raise six children—James Jr., Ray, Juanette, Wanda, Sheila, and Wayne. Ray is Kanye's dad.

James and Fannie West were very spiritual people. Like my family, they attended church every Sunday that the good Lord sent unless they were traveling on the road, moving to yet another city where Pop-Pop had been stationed. Ray tells the story of how they were frequently faced with not being able to stop and rest for the night at motels, not because of money but because of the color of their skin. Pop-Pop was a sergeant in the United States Army, but this did not afford him the right to lodge at the white, racist motels along the way. Not even the restaurants or stores would open their doors to a black family, military or not. Sometimes to keep the family safe, Pop-Pop would drive the car a little distance from the store and walk back to see if he could purchase some bologna and bread and something to drink for his wife and children.

Pop-Pop was a quiet and reserved man who loved his family and his God. Mom-Mom was equally as God-fearing. I never met two finer people than James and Fannie West. They had been married for sixty years. On December 28, 2006, James departed this earth. He had a long illness and it was expected. What wasn't expected was that the very next day, quite suddenly, Fannie joined him. I suppose upon seeing her husband pass, Mom-Mom decided she'd rather leave, too. She'd not been ill and was her same jovial, loving self when I spoke with her the day after Christmas.

"Donda, James is not doing well," she said. "You can see him slipping away." Little did I know that she'd go right behind him. I wonder if she knew. Something in me says she may have. She had lived with this man for sixty years. Had been with him every day, taking care of the home and the kids, except for the rare occasion when she would work outside of the house. Her work was taking care of her six children, all grown now, and her husband. When Pop-Pop left, perhaps she felt her work was done.

That kind of love races through the West family and right through Kanye. Like his parents and grandparents, he is determined, steadfast, persistent, and caring.

This life is about lessons and learning them and sharing them. Kanye had some pretty incredible teachers. He absorbed enough knowledge to be able to take what I thought would be a real negative—dropping out of college—and make it work for him. But again, he had models. Neither my mother nor father was educated beyond the twelfth grade (my dad only went through the sixth—he had to drop out to help his mother provide for their family).

Kanye learned that learning, true education, is in living every day to the fullest. Most of our life lessons cannot be taught in a classroom. Those lessons come from watching and learning from the best—our families. Those lessons don't have to be preached; sometimes they just flow through the blood, in the DNA.

I learned my most important lessons not from school—kindergarten through a doctoral program—but from my dad and my mom, who learned from their mom and dad, who learned from theirs. We are the sum total of the lives our families lived and the lessons they instilled in us—both good and bad.

So before there could be a Kanye, there had to first be his teachers—Chick and Buddy, Mom-Mom and Pop-Pop, mom and dad.

2

Ray West

Our first date was at Greenbriar Mall. Ray West picked me up in his old car. It was pretty beat down. I don't remember the make or model but I do remember that part of the windshield was covered with duct tape and the passenger-side door didn't open, so I had to get in on the driver's side and slide over. But I didn't mind.

I really liked Ray. He was ambitious and had his own photography business. That was part of the attraction. I believe a lot of girls look for guys who are like their dads, especially if they look up to and admire their dads as I did mine. My dad always preached self-sufficiency and being self-employed. Well, Ray worked for himself and he was very smart, creative, and focused. He was not typical, not at all.

We met at Spelman College, where I was working full-time. During those days, I worked three jobs. I taught business writing part-time at Atlanta College of Business. I also filled in for the secretary at a law firm each day while she went to lunch. But my main job, in addition to completing a master's degree at Atlanta University, was working at Spelman as assistant to the head of public relations. I was in charge of recruiting for the school's up-and-coming premed program. Spelman had a huge waiting list, but the vast majority of students came from outside of the Atlanta area. Some people in town viewed the school as snobbish and felt that it overlooked talent in its own backyard. I was sent out to change that perspective. I helped to bring into the school some of the best and brightest in all of Atlanta.

Ray was an independent contractor hired by the PR director to shoot photographs for the new brochures and other promotional items. Sometimes we went out together on recruiting trips. He'd shoot striking black-and-white photographs and I'd tell the counselors and sometimes the students all about the program. He was a master photographer. Everyone loved his work, especially Judy Gebrehewit, my supervisor and the head of public relations. She had fallen in love with the photos he'd taken in South Sea Island. He had won awards for some of those shots. And to look at them made you feel as though you were right there experiencing the culture. Judy raved about his work. Clearly she loved it, almost as much as I would come to love Ray West.

The first time we actually spoke was over the telephone. Judy had set up the introduction and was excited because she thought Ray and I would hit it off. She had told me about this photographer and how great she thought he was. After we spoke, I went into her office.

"Judy, I thought you said Ray West was *black*," I said.

"He is."

"No, he isn't," I said. "Not the man I just talked to!"

Ray sounded *absolutely* white. He didn't just sound like a black man changing his tone and inflections so that his ethnicity would not be readily detected. I could usually tell if that was the case. No, this was the true speaking pattern of Ray West, and he sounded one hundred percent white. As I got to know him, I understood why. He'd been a military kid and had grown up in white neighborhoods. He was born in Tucson, Arizona, but moved from there when he was two. He lived a different experience than most black kids. He even lived overseas for a while. He never even had a black teacher until he went to college. And he never really lived what one might call a black experience.

Suddenly, when he enrolled at the mostly white University of Delaware, the tide turned. For someone who didn't act, speak, dance, dress, or do much of anything else black, how ironic that Ray West was so active, so vocal in the Black Student Government that he was elected its president. I loved to hear him talk about how he snatched the microphone from the president of the university one day at an assembly. I loved that he was militant, fiery, passionate, and above all, very, very smart.

I had never been out with a man like Ray. I was completely captivated. Despite how different we were, there was an instant connection.

Before Ray, I hadn't dated a whole lot. I was very picky about who I decided to spend my time with. When I was in high school I pretended to be cooler than I was. A lot of girls were giving it up, but not me. I didn't have sex until I was entering my second year of college.

Most of the men I had dated were guys who were kind of popular and had smooth pickup lines and a little game. Ray had none of that and I liked that he didn't. He was a bit of a nerd and I liked that, too. He had very little fashion sense, with his JCPenney baggy pants, and I didn't like that—but I felt that would be easy enough to fix. He was honest and sincere and didn't play games, which was perfect for me.

Yes, our first date was at Greenbriar Mall. We had a nice, romantic dinner at Piccadilly Cafeteria. We had both chosen the place. It was quick, clean, and had great food and enough atmosphere for two people who only wanted to look at each other. Afterward, we held hands as we walked about the mall. There was a fountain in the mall where people would make wishes. On that very first real date—we'd been together professionally several times—I threw three pennies in the fountain and wished that Ray West would be my husband.

Three months later we were married.

Looking back, I think God wanted Ray to be the father of my child, which was strange since neither one of us had ever wanted children. I watched both of my older sisters get married and have children when they were very young. I watched their lives go in a direction that was not that appealing to me. My oldest sister finished high school at sixteen and went off to college, but returned home after a couple of years and got married. My other sister married a military man as soon as she finished high school. She finished college after all her kids were grown. I grew up watching them rip and run behind kids and I thought, "Oh no, that will not be my life." I loved children, but I also wanted so much more for myself and I believed at the time that children would prevent me from having it all.

Ray wanted to have it all, too. He and I discussed traveling around the country and around the world. We were going
to have a very nice home, two very nice cars, eat out all the
time, and have fun. We were going to live the good life we
thought all smart, industrious black people like us deserved.
And that's just what we did.

There were so many things about us that weren't as com-
patible as we thought initially. But I didn't process all of that
until much later. When we met, there was an instant attraction. We were best friends. Even when we broke up, we remained friends. Not always friendly, but always friends. Even
when we didn't see eye to eye, we always had chemistry. Lots
and lots of chemistry! Friendship and chemistry are great
bedfellows and led us quickly to the altar.

On January 1, 1973, Ray and I were married in Oklahoma
City. We had a sunrise wedding. Our invitations went out
with a picture of Ray and me on the front with our big Afros.
Behind our silhouette was a sunrise. My mother's sister, Aunt
Ruth, made my dress. It was eggshell white, actually cream.
And it was beautiful—some of Aunt Ruth's best work. She
was known for being one of the best seamstresses in town.
We were married in the church in front of family and friends.
We had a small reception in the church basement, where we
served apple cider and cake, and then we went back to my
parents' house for a big country breakfast—fried chicken,
grits, rice, and biscuits and gravy.

Everything about our wedding was unconventional. We
were unconventional. We didn't have a honeymoon. Ray
booked us a room at the Ramada Inn on Twenty-third Street
in Oklahoma City. We were supposed to have the honeymoon
suite. That's what the man who gave us the room said. But

there was nothing sweet about it. The beds were lumpy and the room was not even clean. Worn and tattered bedspreads, yellowed sheets that were supposed to be white, dirty floors, dark and dingy walls. I actually cried when I saw the room, so Ray said, "Let's go." And we were out of there. We packed up the few things we had unpacked and went to my parents' house, and without even considering spending the night there, we grabbed up as many wedding gifts as we could fit in our rented car and headed back to Atlanta that night to start our lives together.

We settled into my town house. Shortly after starting at Spelman, I had bought my first home. It was a small two-bedroom town house that I'd put $600 down on, and my mortgage payment was $125 a month. I was living there when I met Ray. He had a gorgeous loft apartment in Greenbriar Village. It was huge, with a fireplace. His bedroom overlooked the living room, which had no furniture. In fact, the only room he furnished was his bedroom, which was the only room he really cared about. So he didn't have much to move.

I hated him giving up that apartment, but there was no point in paying rent when I owned a place. We fixed up my town house and made it a home. I was always creative with decorating. And back then, the checkerboard pattern wall I designed using mirrors and twelve-by-twelve corkboard was a real hit. His parents stayed with us once and his mother loved what I had done so much that she went back home and covered one of the walls with cork and mirrors. I was thrilled when I visited their family home in Delaware the first time and saw it. I felt validated. As an artist, Ray was also eclectic and creative. Together we really were quite adept at turning a house into a home. In fact, that's what we did the entire time we were married.

We would drive around suburban Atlanta and dream about where we would live next. If I saw a house I liked, we would buy it. We weren't rich—not on teachers' salaries. He taught photography and media production at Clark College. And I taught English and Speech at Morris Brown College. But we somehow managed to do a lot with the money we did have.

Not long after being in the town home, we moved. A deal came along we didn't want to refuse. It was a four-bedroom, two-story frame house right in the middle of the Cascade area. We loved it even though it needed a little sprucing up. With our skills, we didn't feel that would be hard at all. It wasn't. We bought that big green house on Sandtown Road and put a lot into it. We refinished the kitchen cabinets, replaced the kitchen floor, installed new windows, and carpet, and so on. My mother even came from Oklahoma to help us.

Once she had gone, I remember I had this grand idea to paint one of the four bedrooms red. I thought that would be really hip. Ray didn't think so, but he agreed to let me have my way and we went ahead and hired the painter to get started. Fortunately, the painter knew something I didn't and painted just one wall to show me before continuing. When he showed it to me, though, I turned into Miss Ann instantly.

"Oh no!" I said, almost shouting. "I don't like it! Take it off! Take it off! I don't care what it costs, just take it off!"

I was a real drama queen that day, but Ray humored me. He was a trouper. Less than two years later, we were moving again. Just eight blocks from Sandtown Road, we'd stumbled upon a beautiful house on a quiet, tree-lined street. It was brick and definitely better than our home, or so we thought. Within a week we put our house on the market. It sold almost immediately for a good profit. We had enough money to buy the brick house on the tree-lined street.

The days flew by. No Kanye in sight. Not even a thought of him in either of our minds. Country drives and long talks, no children, were a part of our weekly routine. We loved it.

And it loved us. While driving around an unincorporated part of Atlanta one day, we saw another house and fell in love with it. It was perfect for us. Ray was a nature enthusiast— into natural foods and juicing, before it became popular. He was into eating raw foods and respecting nature. He taught me a lot about that. It sounds funny, but he even taught me to love trees.

Anyway, it was a brick home with a huge basement. It sat on four acres, had a creek, and had plenty of room for a garden. Neither of us was into gardening, but still, the room for one sounded good. Actually, the backyard was practically a forest. It was like living in the wilderness. We had a dog, JT (short for Jive Turkey). We'd found him in a shelter, already trained. And it seemed such a shame not to bring home the little kitten I'd found abandoned in the parking lot at work. For some reason, why I don't know, we called the kitten Mr. Smith. But Mr. Smith ran away for a few weeks and came back pregnant. No more Mr. It was just Ray, Donda, JT, and Mrs. Smith. We were the perfect family.

After one year of teaching English at Morris Brown College, I got the opportunity to study for my doctorate at Auburn University. Ray was always encouraging and didn't ever seem to have a problem with my going away without him to study. Auburn was just a couple of hours away as I remember and we'd planned to see each other every weekend. He would stay home and work as a photographer. He loved his work at the time, but later began to feel that it may not have been wise to turn his hobby into a profession. He was good, I mean brilliant at shooting pictures and at developing them. He even built and equipped a state-of-the art darkroom in the basement of our home. Always wanting to create images from start to finish, Ray preferred doing his own development work rather than sending out the film to be developed. I learned a lot from him about photography. He lived and breathed it in those days. He always talked about composition and about shooting with available light. I was impressed by his knowledge and his talent and very proud to be married to the best photographer, bar none. Everyone thought his work was superior, not just me. I remember objecting vehemently, though, when he wanted to buy a camera lens that cost a thousand dollars. We had a big argument about it, because that was a lot of money back then (heck, it's a lot of money today for a camera lens). I thought the money could have been put to better use. But I didn't win that one. I should have known better than to try and come between Ray West and his camera equipment.

Soon he began shooting photo essays of families. Jenny and Jim Trotter, our neighbors on Sandtown Road, who ultimately became Kanye's first godparents, still had the photo essay he shot of their family displayed proudly on the wall the last time I visited them four or five years ago.

Ray and I were faithful to each other and I believe we trusted each other totally. My faith in him remained even after a little conversation I accidentally heard one day. The phone rang and Ray answered it. While he was still on the phone I casually said, "Who is it?" I wasn't being nosy, neither did I think anything was up. I just wondered who might be calling. One of our friends, I thought. Well, when he told me who it was (some man, he'd said, whose name I don't remember now), for some reason I didn't believe it. So while he was upstairs talking rather low on the phone, I went downstairs and picked up the extension line. It was not a man at all. It was a woman's voice and I heard her clearly. Instantly, I hung up the phone. I don't know why but I wasn't even interested in hearing the conversation. Stranger than that, I wasn't even mad or upset. It crossed my mind then that maybe something was up. Why would he tell me the person was male?

After he got off the phone I calmly confronted him.

"You said that was John [or whatever name he had used]," I said. "But that was the voice of a woman."

Without even hesitating, he confessed. He told me it was some woman named Cynthia. How funny that I remember that name even today, and that was more than thirty years ago. He told me that he couldn't explain why, but he did like her. Nothing had happened between them, he said, and I believed him. Actually, I still do. Maybe I was being foolish or just typically naive, but he'd never lied to me and I didn't think he was lying then.

Ray was visibly disturbed by the whole situation. He had a little conflict going on and I guess he didn't know quite how to feel or what to do. I had no feelings of jealousy or anger, as I'm sure I'd have today if I were married or in a committed relationship with someone and that happened. I just calmly told him that if he liked Cynthia, that sounded like a personal problem to me. He would have to work it out. It wasn't on me. I never felt that our relationship was threatened by her, and really, I'm pretty sure it was not. I loved Ray dearly and I knew he loved me. Maybe that's why I wasn't more affected by the whole situation. I never heard or asked any more about Cynthia. I wasn't even curious. Ray and I spent all our time off work together, so there was never any moment when I was wondering where he was or what he may have been doing. Maybe it was just a passing thing that happened in a short space of our being together. I never met Cynthia, nor did I want to. Maybe it was just a one-call stand.

Some months later I went off to Auburn to study for my degree and left Ray working in Atlanta. As planned, we'd see each other every weekend and we were always elated to be together. After my first year at Auburn, Ray decided to join me. There he would study in the media department and teach medical illustration at Tuskegee Institute, just thirty minutes away from Auburn. He earned a master's in audiovisual studies and media. Like Kanye would come to be, he was a highly visual person and really adept at any kind of work that involved visual representation.

Ray and I had many good times together in Auburn. We lived in married-student housing just two blocks away from the sprawling campus. We enjoyed the friendship of one of my favorite professors, Michael Littleford, and made really good friends with Bart McSwine and his wife, Donna. Bart and Donna were the only black professionals we knew in Auburn. All the other black people we saw were laborers, taking toilet paper out of trees whenever the Tigers would win a football game. The Auburn Tigers were good, though. So a lot of black people stayed employed. Donna and Bart both taught at Tuskegee but lived in Auburn. Ray had met Bart at a health food store and instantly they became friendly. Soon we visited them and Donna and I hit it off, too. They had a baby girl, Myisha. She was beautiful and I was impressed with their vegetarian lifestyle and the way they were raising her.

Life was good in Auburn, but it was not without its down moments. Twice while we were there Ray and I separated. We had begun not to get along very well at all. So funny, however, that every time we'd separate, we'd become best friends again. Once we even found an apartment for Ray in Tuskegee, but he never even stayed in it. In the course of buying sheets, towels, dishes, and everything else he'd need—imagine us doing that together when we'd decided to split up—we began liking each other again and didn't want to spend a night apart. It was crazy. But I'm glad it happened that way. That was before Kanye was born, so had we stayed apart there would never have been a Kanye West.

I completed all my requirements for my degree, except for the dissertation. Ray had already received his master's and it was time to return to Atlanta. We bid good-bye to our friends and professors and headed back home. The plan was for me to finish my writing from Atlanta.

Times were good. To my knowledge, few if any in our circle had it better. I guess those were what some would call the good old days. Ray West was my sweetie, and despite our not getting along at times, we were still crazy about each other. We'd weathered the storm, weathered some things I won't even share here.

We'd come a long way since that fated day we met just three years earlier. Those three coins had paid off a million-fold.

3

And Baby Makes…

I never wanted to have kids. No one ever heard me say growing up that I wanted to have children. Marriage, yes. Children, no. I imagined me and my guy—my husband—traveling around the world and doing things that were absolutely incongruent with the word "babysitter." One of the reasons why Ray and I clicked so well is that he felt the exact same way.

But after a while, the thought of having and raising a baby was for me all-consuming. I was overwhelmed with a feeling that to this day I can't explain. I had made a decision with my head never to have children. But my body and my spirit had other plans. I think it was God selecting Ray and me right then to have the child who would become Kanye West. And despite any of our thoughts to the contrary, nothing was to keep this

pregnancy and birth from happening, not even our initial re-
luctance, or better put, our initial insistence that a kid was
just not in the cards for us. But the script flipped.

My maternal instinct kicked in and went into overdrive.
Still, Ray was not convinced that being a father was what he
wanted to do. He was happy with just the two of us doing
our thing. After all, we had all but vowed not to have kids.
But three years and counting into our marriage, this overwhelming desire in me to get pregnant just would not go
away. So Ray at least began to give some thought to the
idea—partly, I'm sure, because he wanted me to be happy and
partly because I wouldn't and couldn't let it rest.

I had been on birth control pills since Ray and I got together. But this new desire overtook. I have no idea where it
came from. I really don't. I was only twenty-seven when I became pregnant with Kanye, so I know my biological clock
wasn't going haywire. Or maybe it was Mother Nature just
having her way. We are put here to procreate. Who the hell
are we to mess with nature? Well, nature was messing with
me. It was a power greater than I.

One night, I was more emphatic than ever about wanting
to become pregnant and spun into a combination of pleading
and insisting. I told Ray I knew instinctively it was time for
us to have a child despite anything we may have planned or
not planned.

He looked at me, puzzled, and reminded me of what we'd
said.

He said in a voice that was firm but still loving, "I don't
want to have kids."

He wasn't angry. He was just trying to reason with me.

And in that moment, I understood something that had not

been clear to me before. I understood why his paternal instinct had not yet kicked in.

"Donda," he said. "I don't know if I can be a good father. I don't know if it's in me. That's why I don't want to do it."

I totally understood. I didn't know if I would make a good mother, either. I talked with one of my best friends, Jenny Trotter. She and her husband, Jim, had a little girl, SaunToy, at the time, and all the wisdom in the world, it seemed to me. I told Jenny about my secret fears. I told her that for me, becoming a mother was like being asked to perform surgery without going to medical school. I wasn't prepared. Not only that, I, too, was afraid.

Jenny helped that fear dissipate. She had and still has a calming effect on people. Thank God, I was and still am one of them.

"Look at all of these people out here raising kids," she said to me. "It doesn't take a genius. You just have to be a willing, loving person."

She was right. There were a bunch of people having babies who were seemingly less qualified than I was. And most of their children were turning out okay. At least I was starting from a right place—I *wanted* a child and I knew I would love that child. But I didn't want to do it alone.

Ray and I talked more, and soon he became more comfortable with the whole idea. I told him what Jenny had said to me.

"If you want a child, we can have one," he said.

Almost before he could get the words out of his mouth, I got off the pill. Two months later, I was pregnant.

The first weeks after the news were bliss. Ray was very attentive. We still went everywhere together and enjoyed planning and shopping for our unborn child. We even bought an antique rocking chair that I would rock the baby in. I still have it today. Everything was going fine. But as the reality set in, Ray's fears came back with a vengeance.

My closest understanding of that kind of fear was when I was graduating from college. I remember sitting in McVictor dorm on the campus of Virginia Union University a week before graduation, paralyzed with fear. The thought that I would have to be totally grown and fully responsible for my own life brought utter consternation. I would have to pay my own bills, function well in the world, and do so independently. I would have to be the big girl my father always called me.

My parents were very supportive of all of us. But they had a rule: once you were out of college, you were on your own. Of course, emotional and loving support would always be there. But you were expected to make it financially and in every other way once you graduated with that four-year degree. They had worked and saved to educate us. I remember my mother pulling out a big stack of savings bonds she'd been putting away for my college education since I was five or six years old. But now it was graduation time and time for me to make it on my own.

I figured their rule was very fair, until my independence day hit. With graduation fast approaching, I had only a very vague idea of what I would do, where I would go after leaving the environment I had found so nurturing. I was scared as hell when that reality first stared at me. Thinking back, if I'd wanted to go home to Oklahoma City, I knew my daddy would have welcomed it—despite the rule. Both of my parents would have let me come home, especially since I wouldn't have been bringing a baby home for them to raise. They didn't play that.

But I never considered it an option, returning home to my parents' house or to the city I was raised in. I was raised just as I ultimately raised Kanye, to go out in the world, live my life, and tell my truths the way I see them.

I had so many questions. Would I be successful? Could I make my parents proud? Could I make myself proud? I had always been an overachiever. But I was afraid of the unknown. So I knew the place where Ray was and I also knew it was a very real place.

I wanted my husband to be pleased. I felt I couldn't be happy if he wasn't. But I also knew that I couldn't be totally happy if I didn't have a child. I somehow knew that as well as I knew my own name. And even though Ray was off-and-on consumed with unanswered questions about his ability to be an excellent father (he always pursued excellence in everything he did), his questions and fears about fathering lost out to the best decision we ever made.

I thank God that I changed my mind about having a child. I can't imagine what my life would have been without him. Not because he happens to be Kanye West, but because being a mother is for me by far the most rewarding experience I've ever had. Besides life itself, raising Kanye was my greatest blessing. He has brought so much to my life and taught me so much about myself.

As the months wound down and the arrival of our child was imminent, Ray turned into superhusband. He would go to Lamaze classes with me. He had me exercising and eating raw and organic foods. He had me drinking fresh carrot and apple juice. And, from the moment we decided we'd go for it,

I stopped smoking weed. I wanted to provide the healthiest environment I could in which to carry this child. I had fallen in love with him before he was ever conceived. Right before and during my pregnancy, I was probably the healthiest I had ever been. The only thing that got big on me was my stomach.

Ray was totally into it. He photographed every stage of the pregnancy, even me at eight and a half months, riding my bicycle. Once again, we did our unconventional thing. I wouldn't wear maternity clothes because back then you couldn't find anything stylish. I wanted to be fashionable and cute. No baggy, untailored, matronly-looking ensembles for me. So I would wear my jeans and put a hole on the other side and tie a string from the buttonhole to the hole I created, loosening the string as my stomach grew. I wore loose, stylish shirts to cover my stomach as the months progressed.

I knew I was having a boy. Ray said he wanted a girl. I think he just said that so he wouldn't be disappointed in case we had a girl. Or maybe it's that thing that daddies have with their little girls. But I *knew* we were having a boy. We never had an ultrasound, I just felt it. I felt Kanye, too, as he twisted and turned inside me. Boy, did I feel him. He would sometimes poke his elbow into my stomach so hard that I thought he must have been doing gymnastics inside. Many nights he woke me up on the parallel bars or something. But it was always a good feeling no matter how uncomfortable. Ray would get a kick out of feeling my stomach and even conceded after a point that maybe we did have a boy on the way, after all.

The time came when the baby was ready to be born. Ray was pretty cool and collected, as I remember it. He grabbed my already-packed overnight bag and his camera equipment. We got to the hospital and were all ready for the big event, or so we thought. The contractions were ten minutes apart. I was ready. But as it turned out, the baby wasn't. I was to be in labor for a total of thirty-nine hours! I was sweating and pushing and breathing and sweating. And in pain. After the first twelve hours, they sent me home.

"You haven't dilated but three centimeters," the doctor told me. "You can go home and come back when the contractions are five minutes apart."

We went home with no baby. Just labor pains and anticipation. I don't recall having one of those "I curse the day I ever met you, Ray West" moments. Maybe I did. I had prayed and pleaded for this child, but labor pains were no joke. I'm sure I must have looked at this man I loved fiercely as the man who was responsible for all that pain.

Despite all that, I was determined to do this the all-natural way. However, the doctor came to me and said, "Donda, we have to do a C-section."

A C-section?

Here I was juicing, exercising, going to Lamaze classes, doing everything right. I'm thinking the baby should have fallen out. But I guess the baby who would come to be known as Kanye West was going to do things his way even from the womb.

Thirty-nine hours later, I gave in to the drugs that would enable me to bring this child into the world. The doctor said a C-section would be performed if I didn't dilate to ten centimeters. After all of those hours, I managed to dilate only five.

It was disappointing. There would be no birthing room, which was so delicately planned for and eagerly anticipated.

No warm pan of water to submerge the baby in right after he came out. No low lights or candles, the way I wanted to welcome him into the world. Those best-laid plans were derailed.

I would have to take the drugs to have the C-section. I was still conscious, though. I was able to see our beautiful baby boy. He was healthy. The doctor said so without even being asked.

I knew the C-section was a last resort. My doctor was down to earth and encouraged all the natural things like breast-feeding and good nutrition. He even had a midwife work with him and they were both awesome. Ray liked them, too. He always took me to my appointments, so Ray met and talked with them both. Ray was so totally involved in my pregnancy right down to our weekly dinner at the Chinese restaurant where I always ordered butterfly shrimp. How funny now that Kanye does not like seafood.

We lived in Atlanta at the time, but I had chosen to have our baby in a hospital in Douglasville, Georgia, because it offered a birthing room. There, I'd be able to have my husband, my mother (who I learned later was just as content to not be at the actual birth), and even a very close friend or two. The lights would be low in the birthing room so the baby wouldn't undergo as much stress and experience the harsh, bright lights and that clinical feeling immediately upon coming out of the womb.

Ray and I had chosen right—the right doctor, the right hospital, the right classes, the right, healthy lifestyle, and we even selected a birthing room. It was all conducive to having that optimal experience and that perfect baby. We'd been

enormously blessed, despite all of that choosing being for
naught.

Ray ended up being the only person in the room other
than the midwife and the doctor when Kanye was born. We
couldn't have the C-section in the birthing room. But the hospital was small and intimate and the room felt warm to me.

Like everyone does, we had prayed for a healthy baby
with ten fingers and ten toes and all of that. But I also prayed
for him to be brilliant. Brilliant like my dad, who only has a
sixth-grade education but is one of the most intelligent people
I know, a real thinker.

Our prayers were answered. Our baby was healthy *and*
brilliant. Ray was there, camera in hand. He tried to capture
every one of our baby's first moments. He took pictures of everyone who held him in the hospital—the nurses, the doctors.
It was funny. We had all of that time of not wanting kids or
being afraid to have one, and when our son finally came into
the world, there was not a more proud father alive.

My mother came from Oklahoma City to help me out
around the house. But because of the C-section, she ended up
spending more time with me in the hospital. She loved our
actual home, but not where it was situated. My mother didn't
like a bunch of woods where you couldn't see people coming
or going. It made her nervous, so she stayed with me in the
hospital. Only later did she tell me that she wouldn't have
even considered going out there on that four-acre, tree-filled
property while Ray and I stayed in the hospital. I had become
just a little depressed over not getting to have natural child-
birth and not being able to breast-feed for the first week. So
Ray stayed with me. He coached me through labor by having

me think of lakes and trees. He coached me through postpartum depression by reminding me of the tremendous blessing we'd just been given. I remember all of that as though it were yesterday. We were as happy as two people could be.

Only one thing was missing—the perfect name for the perfect baby. With all of the excitement around the pregnancy, we'd never picked out names. So my mother and I began thumbing through this book of African names I'd bought. I was very Afrocentric and so was Ray. We wanted our child to have a name that represented his culture and stood for something. We wanted him to have a strong name.

Mother and I found the name "Kanye" in this book. It was an Ethiopian name that meant "the only one." I knew he would be our only child, set apart, and special.

My mother found his middle name in the Os. She chose "Omari," which means "wise man." Kanye Omari West. Mother pointed out that his initials would be K.O. She liked that it stood for knockout. We asked Ray about the names and he was cool with both Kanye for the first name and Omari as the middle name. So we made it official.

When we got home, Ray was incredible. He did everything but breast-feed. And if he could have found a way to do that, I believe he would have. I couldn't have asked for more support. It was the way I imagined—the way it should have been.

A few months later, we decided to move . . . again. We found a beautiful home in the newly renovated section of West End in Atlanta. Those homes had been gutted and brought back like nothing I'd ever seen. None of that painting over and sprucing up. These homes could rival those in magazines, and at the time, we were the only ones among our friends who could actually manage to land one of those babies. With the sale of our home on the four acres, we had enough money to purchase it.

We put down eight thousand dollars as earnest money, which in those days was nothing to sneeze at. The developers invited us to dinner, where we met all the progressive people who were to be our neighbors. They were mostly, if not all, white. That didn't matter. We'd continue to have all our same friends, and the neighborhood was actually in the hood, not far from everyone we knew and loved. Not far from Jenny and Jim Trotter, who had consented to be Kanye's godparents.

But as fate would have it, before we closed on that house, Ray found this commercial building that would be perfect for his studio. After much thought, the home became history. We could not afford both the home and the photography studio. We even lost our $8,000 earnest money because we'd qualified for the $125,000 mortgage and just didn't want to go forward with the loan. We needed to put the business first. In doing so, we thought that ultimately, we could have anything we wanted. We both believed that when his business took off, we could have as far as we could see. And we saw a lot. It's what we didn't see, I suppose, that made a big difference.

We decided on the commercial building over the beautiful family home in West End. There, Ray could have his studio and expand his business. We would have a loft apartment upstairs and his studio would be downstairs.

Ray worked hard to build his business. He named it RaDonda, which was a combination of both our names. I was very proud of him and what he was doing. For a while he was doing it all while being an attentive daddy, taking care of his family, and trying to build his business into a success.

But as the months rolled on, I noticed Ray spending more and more time with RaDonda and less time with us. I could feel the energy pulling away from us and I didn't like it, so I confronted him.

During a heated discussion he told me that yes, the studio was the most important thing to him. He even confirmed that it came before Kanye and me. What a switch he had made. Long after we'd divorced, though, he told a mutual friend of ours that saying those words and having that attitude were the biggest mistakes he ever made and that he wished he could take those words back. But he couldn't. Those words stung me as much as if he had hauled off and slapped me across my face, because when I looked in his eyes at that moment, I was certain he meant it.

My father always told us that you put God first, family second, and your work third. I didn't mind coming second to God, of course, but I certainly wasn't coming second to Ray's business. Not me and not Kanye.

In that instant, I no longer wanted to stay married to Ray West. Not just because of his perspective on that matter, but because in many ways I was becoming a stranger to myself. It was time to go. Eleven months after Kanye had come into the world, Ray and I separated for the last time. When Kanye was three, we divorced. The divorce was final on August 28, 1980. The only reason I remember the day was because it was Ray's birthday. It was also a rebirth for me.

4

Love Don't Come Easy

Leaving Ray was almost as easy as being with him. I often say that we had a great marriage and a great divorce. When the marriage was working, it was working very well. When it wasn't, it was time to go. There was no bitterness or nastiness, it just was time to go. We had such an amiable breakup that Ray drove me around to find an apartment. I guess we had broken up and reconciled so much that when we did it for the last time, we both knew it was for good.

I probably wouldn't have even filed for divorce if I hadn't planned on leaving Atlanta. I figured when I decided to leave, I needed to make it a clean break. So I filed for full custody and Ray didn't put up much of a fight. He didn't realize what had happened until I was actually moving from Atlanta. I was determined to leave, but there was no way I was going to de-

prive him of seeing his son. I just didn't want him filing abandonment charges against me later, so I had to make it official.

I left Atlanta to start a new life. I moved to Chicago partly
at the encouragement of Larry Lewis. Outside of our romantic
involvement, he showed me how many wonderful opportunities I would have in Chicago. I left Atlanta to pursue some of
those.

I had dated a couple of people after Ray, but Larry was
the first guy I wanted to be serious about. I met him in Atlanta
at the Kool Jazz Festival. He was staying with a friend,
Sheridan, who was also my friend. Larry told Sheridan that
he wanted to meet a nice young lady while he was in Atlanta.
I just happened to be over Sheridan's one day. Larry was out,
but when he walked in, I was sitting at the kitchen table
talking with Sheridan. When Larry and I looked at each other
there were sparks everywhere. I won't say that it was love at
first sight, but there was definitely a connection.

We talked nonstop that night and the whole week or two
he was in Atlanta. Before he left, we were an item. Larry was
smooth but honest, laid-back but outgoing. He was also very
sexy and one of the most fun people I had ever met.

It was not hard to leave Atlanta and head to Chicago. I
had planned to change jobs, maybe even cities, but I just
didn't know where. When all this happened, I knew it was
supposed to unfold that way.

I told my friends and family my plan to move to Chicago
and no one discouraged me. I even drove a truck with our furniture and everything to Chicago by myself. That was the
only time I heard any opposition. Some of my friends didn't
want me to make that trip by myself. But since no one volun-
teered to go with me, I drove those eleven-plus hours to Chi-

cago. I found a place to stay and got settled and came back for Kanye, who was staying with his dad while I was there.

Ray wasn't happy that I was taking Kanye and moving to Chicago. But he didn't put up much of a fight—not even for joint custody. The divorce was final two weeks before I left Atlanta and I had full custody of Kanye. I was ready to embark on the next phase of our life—as a single woman and a single mother.

I had just completed my doctorate in English education. I was young, black, and smart. I could write my own ticket. Before I moved, Larry cut out the yellow pages of the phone book with all the colleges and universities listed and sent me the classifieds from two local newspapers. He had circled things he thought I'd be interested in. I applied to Chicago State and Roosevelt University. I landed both positions. I accepted the one at Chicago State because I wanted to teach in a predominantly black school. I was all set.

Larry Lewis wasn't the primary reason for this change. And I didn't move to Chicago because of any promises we had made each other. I wasn't delusional about our relationship and, quite frankly, I wasn't looking to necessarily get into another serious relationship so soon after my divorce. But I did love Larry, I enjoyed his company, and I needed a change of scenery. So the Windy City suited me just fine.

Larry and I didn't stay together very long. I met him in June, moved to Chicago in late August, went back for Kanye in late September, and four or five months later, Larry and I were history. I only remember when we broke up because by that Valentine's Day we were no longer an item. Although we remain friends to this day.

Kanye was only three years old, and thank goodness he

and Larry never had the time to really bond. I think one of the worst things you can do to your children is have them get close to people—men—and then have those people disappear. It causes a lot of confusion. That's why I was always careful about the men in my life and who I decided to have around my son.

It's not easy being a single woman with a child. You have needs and desires. You want to date and enjoy the company of the opposite sex because after all, you're human. But your child must come first. You cannot have a revolving door of "uncles" and friends coming in and out of your child's life.

I always considered this before I dated any man. Like with Larry, I had options. Ray kept Kanye until I got settled. And after we moved to Chicago, Kanye would spend his summers with Ray and Ray's parents. I had my summers to explore the dating scene. And those three months gave me enough time to know whether a man was worthy of sticking around beyond August, worthy of meeting my son.

A couple of men were worthy. Ulysses Buckley Blakely Jr., or Bucky, was one. I thought he was going to be my last love. He and I had a great relationship. Kanye liked him a lot. He would take Kanye to the park for hours near his apartment building in Evanston. Kanye used to call that park "Bucky's Park." We lived with him for a few months after I returned from India. And we were even going to buy a house together on South Shore Drive, but I think Bucky got cold feet.

That house was supposed to be *our* house. We were to move in there as a family. But love didn't live there anymore. Things had changed between Bucky and me and I could feel it. He never said anything. We didn't have a big blowout argument or anything. He didn't treat Kanye any differently.

Isn't that a cute baby? It's me!

Me in The Unwicked Witch at Virginia Union University. A star is born!

Baby Kanye with his father, Ray.

Ray's parents

James and Fannie West

I'm 8½ months pregnant and still riding my bike.

"A baby is God's opinion that the world should go on."
— Carl Sandburg

We're having a shower to celebrate
the coming of a new life.
Please join us!

Sunday, May 22, 1977, at 4:00 p.m.
1304 Boulevard Lorraine, S.W.
Atlanta, Georgia 30311

(given by Janis Epps for Donda West)

Kanye and Mom-mom-Ray's mom, Fannie West.

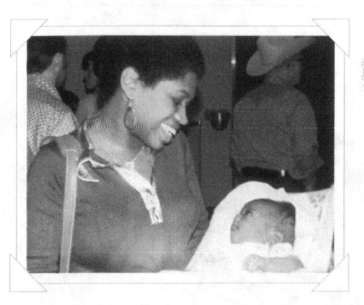

Look at that face! Kanye at three months old.
You couldn't find a more proud mother.

My parents

Portwood and Lucille Williams.

Love the 'do!

*Ray West.
Kanye's dad.*

The Williams Family
Mother and Daddy (center), me (left),
Portwood, Jr. (back), Klaye (next to Mother),
Shirley (behind Klaye).

Kanye, a pretty sharp dresser at two. Love that blue tie!

Great baby daddy potential, don't you think? Pre-school photo at Chicago State University. He was New York-bound even then.

Kanye at a car show in Chicago. I wished I had dressed him better that day. He loved nice cars, even then.

above: Kanye at ten chillin' at a resort in Thailand.

above: Kanye cooling his feet in Thailand. He almost drowned in that ocean. left: Donda on Yellow Mountain in China.

Kanye with a bike on the beach.

Kanye clowning around on the beach in Thailand.

Kanye taking a break on the steps of Huang Shan (Yellow Mountain) in the eastern part of China. I couldn't walk after climbing that mountain. But Kanye was fine.

Kanye at Chungking House in Hong Kong. The rooms were just $11 a night.

Me and Kanye eating Chinese food at a local hangout in China. Check out the chopstick skills.

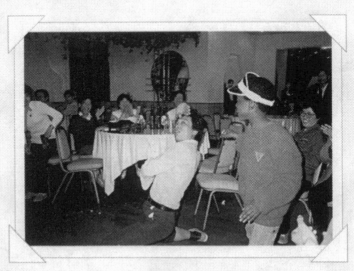

Kanye watching the entertainment at a dinner in China.

Me in Poland.

Me at a resort in Indiana.

Kanye with Lucien,
a fellow rapper.

Kanye with
rapper friends,
Gene and Lucien.

Me with my best friend, Glenda.

Check me out. One profile is worth a thousand words.

Yes. I have some style. too!

Smiling for the camera.

Me entertaining at home.

The Roses Chick and Buddy's 65th anniversary party.

Things were just different between us. The love didn't feel the same.

I was torn at the time. I really wanted that house and I couldn't afford it by myself. But there was no way I could see myself staying with a man because I thought I needed him or putting Bucky into a situation that I knew he didn't want. I believe he would have moved into that house with me had I pressed the issue. But I wasn't going to press the issue.

I had to do something. But I really didn't know what to do. One day I got on the bus and what should I see in the seat I was about to take? A sign that read: BAN THE BUCK! The Chicago Transit Authority was requiring all passengers to use correct change. Back then a bus ride was only a quarter. There were ads everywhere to "Ban the Buck!" I thought it was a sign for me to kick Bucky to the curb. I had prayed for a sign, but I never imagined God would take me so literally.

It was time for me to ban the Buck. I don't think Bucky minded at all. Actually, I think he was relieved. He was not the kind of man who would have wanted to bail out of the relationship. He was a kind, loving, generous, responsible man. But it was time to move on.

After Bucky, there was Tony. Kanye actually hooked me up with him. I was taking Kanye voting with me at our local place. I saw this handsome man—he was tall, six foot four (I am all of five four). Before we voted, Kanye tugged on me to check this guy out. I already had. We went in to vote (I always took Kanye in the booth with me because I wanted to expose him to the process). When we were finished, the man was gone.

I decided to walk up the street a bit. They were building some town houses there and they had a few models open.

Who would we bump into there? The man from the voting facility. I wasn't the kind of woman to ever make a move, so I just went about my business, looking at the models. When I finished, I started to head home. Tony, being a man, wanted to check out the garages. Kanye saw an opportunity. Grabbing me by the hand, Kanye pulled me in Tony's direction.

"Mom, he went that way!" Kanye said.

I was so amused. Here was this little six-year-old trying to hook me up. Kanye wanted me to have somebody. I think he never wanted me to be alone. I don't know what it was about Tony that caught Kanye's eye, but he was being rather insistent that we go in Tony's direction. I kept heading toward home, though, not interested in seeing the garages. But Kanye carried on, wanting me to follow this man. Tony ended up catching up to us. And we struck up a conversation. Kanye stood there just as nice as he could be. It was as though he were saying, "I'm a good boy, see. No trouble at all!"

Any other time, Kanye would have been ready to go, fidgety, in fact. But he waited patiently. Tony asked for my number but I told him I'd take his instead. Rarely, if ever, would I give my number to a man. I called Tony a week later and we ended up dating for a couple of years. Kanye liked Tony. He especially liked that Tony rode motorcycles. Kanye was so small then, I dared not let him ride on the back with Tony. But it was a good relationship while it lasted.

Scotty was the closest I came to actually marrying again. Kanye called him "my almost stepdad."

I met Scotty at my going-away party in my backyard. Kanye and I were leaving for China for a year and Scotty tagged along with my best friend, who lived in his building. He had locked himself out of the apartment that evening; she saw him in the lobby and invited him to come with her to my party.

Nothing really got started then. We talked a little but I didn't make much of it. But I heard that he asked about me for the entire year I was in China (I guess I made an impression, huh?).

When we got back, Scotty asked me out. After that first date, it was on. We were together for six years. What impressed me was that he was an old-fashioned gentleman, meaning he knew how to make a woman feel like a lady. He was a sharp dresser, interesting to talk to, and very progressive-minded. And he was a whole lot of fun.

He was an auto mechanic teacher at a local high school and was involved in lots of activities through the teachers union. But I really liked that the students he taught were all very fond of him. They loved him dearly. Some of the boys would come up to him during football games or wherever we were just to speak to him. Some who had graduated still made it a point to come and pay their respects to Mr. Willie Scott.

We lived together for a few years. But our relationship ended primarily over a dispute over how I should raise Kanye. Some of his old-fashioned, stern schoolteacher ways just weren't congruent with the way I wanted to raise my son. I did respect, however, Scotty's point of view, and never interfered (at least not openly) with the way he disciplined Kanye. I wanted that strong male influence for Kanye on a daily basis. But Scotty seemed more interested in punishment than discipline and exchange.

I always believed that children aren't these silent slaves who should be seen and not heard, who should obey and nothing more. I believed that you should communicate with your child and that if you're a good parent, your child will obey you because he respects you, not because he's afraid of you.

Scotty was from the fear-and-awe school of parenting. He was one to focus more on taking away things and privileges—for example, if Kanye hadn't cleaned the tub well enough or mopped the kitchen floor to Scotty's satisfaction.

While that kind of parenting has its place, I was more interested in nurturing the creative side of Kanye, making sure that he was widely exposed and even heavily indulged. Scotty felt that I was too lenient. Scotty would say the few times I came to Kanye's defense about a chore left undone, "You're going to fuck him up!"

Scotty thought I was spoiling Kanye, ruining him, by letting him get away with any one small thing. I learned later that his military stance was, in fact, good for Kanye. But still, enough was enough. The breaking point for us came the day there was a piece of paper on the lawn.

It was Kanye's job to keep the lawn free of debris. And somehow a piece of paper ended up on the lawn. Scotty lost it. I believe he overreacted. It was one thing to discipline a child, it was quite another to be overbearing. I knew then it was time to go.

Kanye and Scotty had their share of run-ins by this time and I felt Kanye was growing unhappy being around him. I had caught Kanye sitting at the dining room table almost in tears. He and Scotty weren't getting along that day. I asked him what was wrong.

"If you love him, Mom, stay with him," Kanye said. "I'll be out of the house one day."

"But what will you do now?" I asked Kanye.

"I guess I'll just go live with my dad," he said, wiping the tears from his eyes.

That was it. Kanye never cried and I knew he didn't want to go live with his dad. He was content just staying with him for the summers, but for good? That's not what he wanted. If I believed that Kanye truly preferred to live with his dad, I would have been devastated, but I would have let him go. But he was only asking to leave because he was unhappy living with Scotty.

There was no way in hell I was going to send Kanye off to stay with his dad just so that Scotty and I could be together. What Kanye says in the song is true. I "never put no man over" him and I wasn't about to start then.

Not long after that day Kanye sat at the table teary-eyed, I took my child and moved out. I still loved Scotty. But love was not enough—not enough to make my child unhappy.

I'm glad I went through those loves and exposed Kanye to all of it—the good, the bad, and the ugly. There were some lessons there for him, too. One of them was that love doesn't come easy. When you know that truth, perhaps you're more apt to treasure it when you find it and you're less likely to jump into a relationship without thought and care.

My greatest love, though, which outweighed any love I could have for any man, was for my child. Women must realize that their first responsibility, their first consideration must be for their children. Too many women put a man before their child and that's wrong. Men come and go, but your children will be your children forever.

The one thing your child must know is that he is loved above all else. You give him security and confidence when you let him know that no matter what, he will always be loved. That doesn't mean that you stop your life. That doesn't mean that you live like a nun. That doesn't mean that you aren't tough and that you don't discipline your child and even punish him when necessary. What it means is that you love him unconditionally, and you let him know that the love you have will never fade. The love for your child is not like a love for any man—that may fade at any time. This love is eternal.

And that's what I let Kanye know—that my love for him was unconditional and eternal.

5

"Hey Mama!"

My mama told me go to school, get your doctorate
But still supported me when I did the opposite
KANYE WEST, "Hey Mama," *Late Registration*

The first time I actually saw the term "mama's boy" connected to Kanye was in a Chicago newspaper in 2005. It was in the headline of a cover story for the entertainment section. The headline read: "Kanye: A Mama's Boy After All."

I didn't like the reference at first, but the actual story was quite glowing. I was very proud of it and so was Kanye. When he was asked about me in an interview he said, "My mama's my best friend. I talk to her every day."

It's no secret that Kanye and I are really, really close and always have been. I have accompanied him to awards shows, been his general manager, and am now the CEO of his parent company, Super Good, as well as the chair of the Kanye West Foundation.

If asked before the article appeared to define the phrase

"mama's boy," I probably would have said it was a pejorative, a description of a male child who was too tied to his mama and who'd never quite come into his own. But that was a connotative meaning that was totally and ultimately inaccurate. Now I think of the phrase in very positive ways. That you're a mama's boy doesn't mean you're not a man. Kanye is very much his own man. I recall him saying in an interview, "I'm not tough, but I am strong." He can love his mother and still be a strong man.

I really don't ever remember that mama's boy moniker being a problem with Kanye when he was growing up. And I was always very involved in his life. I worked in one of his day care centers, and later, I was always volunteering at his school. Whether it was attending a PTA meeting, chaperoning kids on a field trip, or editing the parent-teacher newsletter, I was always there. It never seemed to bother him. I was supportive and I believe he appreciated it. It was a source of comfort, knowing that I would always be there.

I remember one time when he was just a toddler, I had to work a long stretch at the school. I was teaching at Morris Brown College in Atlanta, Georgia, then and had to do some advising after a full day of classes. This was at a time when we definitely needed extra money. It was a necessity, not a luxury, and I just couldn't afford not to make that extra money advising for a couple of weeks.

I'd dropped Kanye off at about seven in the morning and didn't pick him up until ten that evening. Boy, was he mad at me. He had his little arms folded and wouldn't say a word.

"We can get some ice cream," I said as we were driving home. I was feeling really badly and trying to bribe him into forgiving me. Kanye wasn't having it, though. He turned his head toward the window away from me and continued to sulk. I tried everything I could to win his favor, but to no avail. Finally, I became a little frustrated and said, "Well, just forget you, then!"

Instantly he unfolded those little arms and burst into laughter. I was stunned that a baby—he was scarcely more than a year old—could hold his own like that. I could not believe he was so focused and so determined not to give in. Never had I met a kid who could not be snapped out of his mood with the offer of an ice cream cone. Not Kanye. He felt that I had abandoned him and he wanted me to know it. I think he wanted to pay me back, and he surely did. I was a little taken aback by the whole ordeal. But I was more relieved than anything that he had finally forgiven me.

I always hated the thought of disappointing any child in any way. That time it couldn't be helped, though, and I was as sad as he was. Except for punishing him when he needed to be punished, I don't think I ever disappointed him ever again after that.

Like the song says, Kanye was just three years old when he and I moved to the Chi. I'd gone to Chicago a month before I went back to Atlanta to get him from his dad. I needed to find a place that would be affordable, safe, and ideal for a single parent raising a young boy in Chicago. That was not the easiest task, partly because of my limited budget and my limitless taste. And partly because in the nicer places, children were not always welcome.

I persisted, though, and found a wonderful place near Chicago State University, where I'd already begun teaching, and also near Professional Playhouse Daycare, where I'd enroll Kanye in school. The landlords, a very nice lady and her husband, had at first turned me down. They explained that while they loved children, they felt that having one in their three-flat building would attract other children and that the yard would always be full of them.

They themselves occupied the first floor and another single lady without any children lived on the second. I loved the place the moment I looked at it and thought it to be just perfect for Kanye and me. So I insisted that having Kanye there would not attract a single kid. After all, he was just three years old and I had no intention of letting him go out to play without me. Still they turned me down. How glad I was when they called back to tell me I could have the apartment. The tenant they had chosen had not worked out for some reason. So they called Chicago State to verify my employment and ended up being rather impressed with me.

They complimented me on having just earned the doctorate degree and on becoming an instructor at the neighborhood university. They said they wanted smart people in their building and that if we still wanted it, the apartment was ours. Within one week we moved in. Kanye had his own room and there was a living room, large dining room, full kitchen, and an enclosed back porch. My room was right next to his and we both felt very comfortable in our new home. It was a godsend—just like the job, just like Larry Lewis, the man who'd been the catalyst for our moving from Atlanta, and just like Chicago itself, a city I'd vowed never to live in but came to embrace as my favorite city in the world.

I loved working at Chicago State and I think Kanye was proud of me even then. It was a new start for us and we both were very happy. In one year, I purchased a home for us in South Shore. Mama would rent no more and Kanye would have his own backyard. He was a little older and kids could come over if they wanted to. I didn't know it, but South Shore, and especially South Shore Drive, where we lived, was considered "the shit," a prestigious area in a coveted part of town. We were within walking distance of Lake Michigan and our backyard backed up to Rainbow Park. It's in the kitchen of that house that Kanye talks about kneeling on the kitchen floor and saying "Mama, I'm gonna love you 'til you don't hurt no more." He had seen me fall in love only to be disappointed and had never forgotten, even up to the day he wrote "Hey Mama."

Lots happened in those eight years we lived on South Shore Drive. I enrolled Kanye in preschool at Chicago State University. Nothing was wrong with Professional Playhouse, where he started when we first left Atlanta. But since I was teaching at CSU and had waited for a year for the preschool there to prove itself worthy (it was brand-new and I preferred to wait until its second year of operation for them to work out their kinks), I decided to take Kanye out of Professional Playhouse and enroll him in the school on the campus where I taught. It would be a little more convenient for me and I could check on him throughout the day. It turned out to be an excellent school where the director and teachers were caring and nurturing—one where the children learned something new every day and all the parents were required to be actively involved.

In no time, Kanye was ready to enroll in kindergarten. His teachers told me that academically, he was fine, even gifted. But socially, they thought he needed some help. They told me Kanye did not work well with others, that he was self-centered and needed another year there to adjust to public school. There was a kindergarten at the preschool and for about half a second I considered whether I would take their advice. The answer came quickly, though. When I debated leaving him there at nearly three hundred dollars a month or finding a good public school and seeing to it that he worked well with others, I chose the latter. The money wasn't the major factor (although it was a factor). I was confident that Kanye would do just fine in regular kindergarten.

I checked out Powell School on South Shore Drive. All the kids in the neighborhood were going there and it was only four blocks down the street. Named for Adam Clayton Powell, someone who I'd long admired, it did not quite measure up to the standards I had in mind for the school Kanye would attend. Kindergarten would be his entry into real school, and like many of the mothers I had met at his preschool, I was hell-bent on making sure he'd get into one of the best schools in the city.

For a minute, I considered a school in Lincoln Park. It was in Near North and quite a distance from the house. There would be no way for him to get there except my taking him. That was secondary, though, because the school sounded so great. The curriculum allowed for applied teaching and hands-on learning. I knew the value of both. I was impressed with the activities and the many field excursions the kids were afforded. But what I did not like, besides the long drive on icy winter mornings, was that there were no other black kids at the school. While I applauded diversity, I did not want Kanye to be the only "diverse" kid there. So I continued my search for another school.

Just in the nick of time, another mother of one of the preschoolers, Beverly, told me about Vanderpoel Magnet School. She told me it was excellent and known for teaching the arts. After talking with her and visiting the school, I was sold. Mr. Olsen, the principal, Ms. Wooten, the vice principal, and Ms. Morgan, the music teacher, all stood out to me as the kinds of educators I wanted to influence Kanye. So did Ms. Murry, the kindergarten teacher, who was also patient and kind.

Our only problem was that we missed the deadline for applying. Here is where I knew I'd have to do a little handi-work and call on someone I knew at the board of ed for a favor. One more problem: I was fairly new to the city and really didn't know many people, nor was I due any favors. But I figured I was young, gifted, black, degreed, and a professor of English at Chicago State University. Surely there would be a way to get some consideration. We'd only missed the deadline by a couple of days and the school still had a couple of spaces. Mama strikes again! I'd get Kanye in that school or bust.

I asked the provost at my university to help me and I suppose he did. I don't really know what happened. I just know that within a couple of days of visiting the school, Kanye was invited to apply. In those days, kids weren't selected to attend magnet schools by lottery, as they would be in subsequent years. A battery of tests were given, and fortunately Kanye did well on them all. I couldn't help but be amused when they asked him to draw a man. Kanye told them he'd draw a football player, but they told him he couldn't do that. They wanted him simply to draw a man. I learned later that there was a scoring system based on the detail included, and I guess the test did not allow for a picture of a football player.

Kanye said he'd draw a man, but he was going to put him in a football suit. They just looked at one another and said okay. Kanye drew his football player and passed the test in flying colors. My baby was in Vanderpoel and there he would stay until he graduated from eighth grade.

It was during those times that I "work[ed] late nights just to keep on the lights." And I "got [him] training wheels so [he] could keep on [his] bike." "[I] would give anything in this world/Michael Jackson leather and a glove, but didn't give [him] a curl."

Not everything was perfect during those years, and although Kanye was a good kid, he got into his share of devilment. I'll never forget the day he took the X-rated magazine to school. He was passing it around for the other boys to see and the teacher caught him. I've never been so embarrassed as the day I had to go to the school and face Ms. Wooten. She was so tough that I was almost afraid of her.

"Look what Kanye brought to school," she said, showing me the magazine. I wanted to crawl through any hole in the floor. And if his taking it to school wasn't bad enough, she told me that when she asked him where he'd gotten the magazine, he said, "From my mother's closet."

I could have killed him. I didn't know what to say. And to this day, I don't know what I did say. Everything seems somewhat of a blur after that, until I had Kanye in the car and proceeded to yell at him like I'd never done before. Before I knew it, I'd lost my temper and smacked him across his face. The bad thing about that is that I wasn't even sorry for it. I dared him to ever do such a thing again, and I think it took me hours, if not days, to cool down.

That wasn't the last time Kanye would get caught with his pants down, at least figuratively speaking. He had graduated from Vanderpoel and gone on to Polaris High. I decided to borrow his VCR to look at a movie because the one in our room (Scotty's and mine) was on the blink. To my surprise and utter dismay, Kanye had an X-rated tape in it that in my opinion was too graphic for the most mature adult, much less a fourteen-year-old boy. It was triple-X-rated and I was mad as hell about it. He'd gotten it from one of the boys at school and it seems they had been taking turns watching it. I was so angry that I didn't say a word for two days. I couldn't because I didn't know what to say or what to do.

I did take the tape out so that he'd sweat a little (or hopefully a lot), wondering what had happened to it. When I regained my composure, I confronted him. By this time I had already decided what the consequences would be. I knew that ranting and raving would not deter this behavior. I knew that making him promise never to watch such a thing again would only make him lie to me. So what could I do that might have some positive impact? What could I say that might result in something productive? I wanted to be the mama of mamas, and yet, in this situation I found myself speechless.

In that two days of not mentioning a word to Kanye, it came to me what I should do. Calmly, I approached him with the tape in my hand and said, "What is this?" It was the moment he'd been dreading, I'm sure, and the moment I'd begun to anticipate. To my surprise he said quite openly, "It's a tape I got from Johnny [not his real name]."

"What were you doing with it in your VCR?" I asked him.

With his head down, he told me he'd been watching it. I don't know what I expected him to say. I'd always raised him to tell the truth, and somehow, I wished then that he'd thought of a lie I could believe. Of course, I knew he'd been watching it. Why else would it have been there? Thankfully, I had taken a moment to reflect on the whole matter and to ask for guidance in confronting him. The direction had come and to this day I know it was better to have done what I did than to have ranted and raved and forbidden his actions. I asked him if he thought it was healthy for young teenaged boys to look at X-rated movies. I continued with a series of other related questions. I was surprised by the maturity of some of his answers and annoyed by the flipness of others. In the end, however, I required him to do a full-blown research paper complete with footnotes and bibliography. I gave him three topics to choose from, but I only remember the topic he chose; "The Impact of Watching X-Rated Movies on a Teen-aged Boy."

Until he finished that paper to my satisfaction, there was to be no television, no going to play basketball, no friends over, or any other activity. Needless to say, he worked on the paper consistently and finished a decent paper in a pretty short time. I corrected it as though he were in one of my college classes, allowing no misspellings and requiring correct documentation. I don't believe it deterred an affinity for such videos. But I do know he learned quite a bit about how to do a research paper and I thought that in itself to be a very valuable lesson.

In Kanye's earlier years, I had friends and quite a few relatives who thought I was too permissive with Kanye. They felt I didn't discipline him enough, that I allowed him to do and say things that he shouldn't. I never believed you should stifle children and beat them into submission for the sake of your ease and comfort. I always wanted my son to feel free to express himself. Of course, there needed to be boundaries and I was always pleased to know that if I told Kanye I didn't like something, he would fix it.

I always wanted him to be his own person—not some cookie cutout of me or his dad. I didn't put many restrictions on Kanye.

He used to call my sister Klaye instead of Aunt Klaye. I didn't have a problem with it because that's what I called her. I guess being the youngest and having nieces and nephews close to my age, and having them sometimes call me by my first name instead of Aunt Donda, made it cool.

But some family and friends did not seem to like that at all. After all, in a traditional black family, there are these rules. You have to call people Miss Whatever-their-name-is. You can use either the first name or last name, but if she is an elder, you have to call her Miss Jones or Miss Mae. And for men, it's Mr. Smith or Mr. Paul. You can't call older people by their first names. It's a show of disrespect. And I understand that. I may not agree with it, but that's the way it is. So I had to talk to Kanye about that. We live in a world with people and you can't always do things your way just because you feel it's right. You have to be considerate of how other people see things, too.

Kanye did things like that, not to be disrespectful but because he couldn't see why it had to be done the way everyone else did it. It was part of his wanting to stand out. But sometimes he would get beside himself. He'd be a little more grown than even I, the permissive one, would allow.

We'd moved to Chicago during the summer. But before our move I'd visited on a couple of occasions to interview for jobs and get acclimated to the city. On one of those visits, I'd made a few friends. One of them was Linda Pruitt (whose name is Jahon Rashid today). I met her through Larry Lewis, the guy I met at the Kool Jazz Festival in Atlanta and who was responsible for me being in Chicago. His best friend, Frank, was either going with or married to Linda. I don't remember which now. Instantly, she and I hit it off and became best friends.

It would be a while before Linda spent any real time around Kanye. She'd just seen him briefly here and there. He was very young then and very likely did not remember her at all. One summer after Kanye had just come home to Chicago after spending the summer with his dad, Linda came over for a visit.

Kanye ran to the door, opened it, saw Linda, and said, "Who are you?!" Not "Hello." Not "May I help you?" Just "Who are you?!"

He couldn't have been more than five years old. Linda was not amused.

"Boy, I'm your mother's best friend!" she said. "You better get out of the way and let me in this house!"

I didn't know until years later (actually, after Kanye had made it) that she remembered that day well. She confessed, "I'm going to tell you, I thought Kanye was a spoiled, snot-nosed kid who would grow up to be trouble."

She never told me that then. But had I heard him speak to her in that manner, I would have put him in his place. Looking back, I could understand why she thought as she did.

But back then, I couldn't see it. I guess I was totally blinded. I thought just about everything he did was brilliant and wonderful.

I guess he was very much my boy—mama's boy. What was wrong to others was not always wrong to me.

I appreciated that Kanye saw things differently. He never thought inside of the box. He began to draw when he was three years old, and I bought him a huge box of Crayolas. You know, the one with the sharpener in the back. I think it was a box of sixty-four. Even then, his talent stood out. He drew things that kids who were twice his age couldn't draw. He drew people—real people, not stick people. I was impressed by it.

I remember having a conversation with him about colors and how a banana is supposed to be yellow and an orange should be orange. But he rarely made things the "right" color, not unless he wanted to. He would make the banana purple and the orange blue. I didn't tell him it was wrong. That was the way he wanted to see it. He knew that a banana was actually yellow, but he wanted to make it purple and I didn't argue with him.

When he was six, my sister and brother-in-law took him to a lake. There were ducks there just quacking away. Kanye took exception to the way the ducks were quacking.

"That's not the way that's supposed to sound," he said, and started quacking the way he thought it should be. Now, these were real ducks quacking and he felt like they were doing it wrong. In his mind it should have sounded a different way. He was adamant that the ducks were quacking wrong. Kanye had a distinct perspective. He always had his own spin on things. I never criticized him for it. I figured I would just nurture the creativity.

Why does a banana have to be yellow? Maybe the ducks were quacking wrong. I never thought when he grew up that he would be looking for a purple banana.

It's ironic he'd be considered a mama's boy when he was so independent of me. All kids need their mothers and there is a huge amount of dependence that most will never even acknowledge. Whether or not he depended on me openly, I just wanted Kanye to know that I loved him unconditionally and that it was critically important for him to display respect for himself and others.

Respect has always been a big thing in our house—not just being respected but learning how to respect. And because Kanye has a high regard for me, it makes him a better man. He has never denied being a mama's boy. And even in the tough world of rap, that respect he has for me shines through in the way those around Kanye treat me. And I appreciate that.

Whether it's Jay-Z or Ludacris or Nelly or John Legend or Common—or Don C., Kanye's road manager; Gee, his manager; Ibn, his barber; or any of his many friends—they all walk in with so much respect. And I know it's because of how Kanye treats me. I don't know how they act around others. I suspect they display that same level of respect. In fact, I know they do because I know some of their mothers. But Kanye has set the tone for how I should be treated. And it's always with utmost respect.

When he was younger and he'd play one of his songs for me, he'd always turn down the volume on any part with profanity. Now, I knew Kanye cursed and not all the words in his music were from his Sunday school class. But I liked that he felt it appropriate to spare me from some of the lyrics. It was all about respect. Now that I've become a true hip-hop mom and Kanye is well beyond his teen years, he knows I don't mind hearing all the lyrics and that, in fact, I prefer to. There is no need to turn the volume down. The respect remains and I know it.

That children should have respect for themselves and for their parents is a given. It's something that I required of Kanye and that my parents required of me. Yet frequently, that's not how it is. Some may say it's phony to avoid certain behaviors in front of a parent or vice versa. But I've always believed it's the right thing to do. Admittedly, some things become age appropriate, like Kanye not needing to edit for me the profanity in his music. But other behavior may or may not ever be appropriate. What one does with one's peers is not necessarily the respectful thing to do in all situations. I know Kanye has intuited this, as I've never spoken on it to him. I never had to. Some things are taught by setting an example.

The whole respect thing is declining. Permissive as I was when Kanye was a child, and cool as I fancy myself now that he's an adult, he has never disrespected me. I'm concerned that across the board, however, that may be the exception rather than the rule. What greater evidence is there than the way some children treat and act around their parents? It's not necessary to watch Jerry Springer or other such shows to know that this is true. We need but to look around us. Disrespect is running rampant and it didn't start yesterday.

I remember when I was in graduate school, my roommate, an undergraduate, was growing impatient about something. I heard her say, not even under her breath, "I wish that bitch would come on!"

"Who are you talking about?" I asked her.

And without hesitation she replied, "My mother!"

Now, I could never imagine *thinking* about referring to my mother as a bitch, much less actually doing it. It would never enter my mind no matter what the situation. But in some households it is commonplace, a phenomenon that to me is as disturbing as it is damaging.

If you can even fix your lips to call your mother a bitch— even if she is one—you're not only disrespecting her, you're also disrespecting yourself.

But many kids don't know any better because parents aren't stepping up and teaching them better.

Not long ago, one of my little twin nephews came to visit his grandmother. They haven't spent much time with our side of the family. But, of course, we love them dearly. At five years old, they are the cutest little boys you'll ever see—Hollywood cute. They are also sweet and well behaved. Nevertheless, there was music playing that I guess one of the twins didn't like. He said, "Can you turn that *damn* thing down! It's annoying me!"

Everyone in the room just stopped. We come from one of those families where that just wasn't allowed. When we were coming up, if an adult was in a room and wanted to curse, he or she had to spell it out or use pig Latin. But my little nephews hadn't a clue that to use the word "damn" at age five was not going on. Not even I would allow such language raising Kanye—not to my face or anywhere within earshot.

"Justin, we don't talk like that," my niece said to him in a calm voice. She didn't go off on him and scream and yell.

He looked up and said, "Oh, okay." It didn't dawn on him

that it was inappropriate for him to say that. He was never taught that. But he learned that night.

There are some old-fashioned values I insisted on that could serve us well today. People talk about back-to-basics—reading, writing, and arithmetic. But there are some basic values we must return to as well, not the least of which is respect. Honesty, integrity, and a strong work ethic were traits I knew had to be instilled in Kanye. He wasn't going to learn them through osmosis. And if I, his dad, his grandparents, aunts, uncles, and any adult he was allowed to be around did not teach him, the streets and impolite TV certainly weren't going to.

It's not rocket science to conclude that we spend too much time and money on things that aren't as important as teaching our kids the basics. We build space stations on the moon—and neglect the fundamentals. As Kanye was growing up (and now, as well, of course), people actually took the lives of other human beings daily and thought nothing of it. Now, decades later, there isn't a night that goes by that someone isn't killed or injured because someone "dissed" them. We have come so far and our ancestors have sacrificed so much. If we fail to keep our children mindful of this, disrespect will continue to run rampant.

When Kanye was very young, I began teaching him to love himself. It's something I felt I must consciously do. The low self-esteem he was bound to take on if he looked to the media for validation would only serve to cripple him and make him question himself into oblivion. As a black man and as a man period, he would need to be strong. This would not happen if he learned to hate rather than love himself. And in a society where our legacy is surely the love of our forefathers but also the hate of slave masters, it is imperative that parents consciously teach the love of self, the courage of Malcolm, the wisdom of Martin, the tenacity of Marcus.

I believe that unless combated, self-hate is easy to develop and nearly impossible to shed. One of the best ways to teach a child to love himself and others is to love that child with all your might. Perhaps it is the only way. If you don't know that you are loved, how can you possibly have a conscience? How can you care about another person? It's so basic. Yet we almost miss it. But if you know you are loved and are taught to love by those who raise and nurture you, you have what's fundamental to a well-adjusted and happy life.

I spent a few days in Spain in 2006, and I met a guy there who grew up with very little. Economically, he was deprived as a child and didn't always know how he was going to survive from day to day. Today he is highly successful financially and otherwise. I asked him what made the difference for him.

"Unconditional love," he told me. His daddy left when he was five months old, but his mother was right there. No matter what they lacked or whether they were able to eat on a given day, he knew his mother loved him every single moment of his life. For him, her loving him unconditionally made all the difference.

I would say that anyone who grows up to be a reasonably well-adjusted, fulfilled individual has to have had someone there—a mother, a father, a teacher, a pastor, a friend or other family member—who really loved them and made it known. If you don't get that, you can't grow up feeling good inside even if you defy the odds and become successful. If you get too much love, maybe you'll be called a mama's boy. But that isn't the worst thing in the world, is it?

6

I'll Fly Away: From Chi-town to Shanghai

I would give Kanye the world if I could. But I guess I did the next best thing—I exposed him to the world. I knew that more than money, clothes, and things, exposure to new things, exposure to different things, is perhaps the best gift you can give your child. My goal was to show Kanye the world so that he could make up his own mind how things were—but he would do it from experience.

Kanye had his first plane ride when he was just eight weeks old. We flew to Oklahoma City to attend my ten-year high school class reunion. This was 1977 and I was feeling pretty good. I had earned a couple of degrees, had traveled a good bit and met people from all over the country and the world. But what I was most proud of was Kanye Omari West.

My mother kept Kanye while I attended most of the

events. But I had him strapped in a carrier to my front for a few gatherings. He was a great baby. At our class dinner, I got the prize for having the youngest child. I kept that prize—a baby bottle and two pacifiers—for years. We didn't have much use for the pacifiers, though, because Kanye had been sucking those two fingers since he came out of the womb and that's all he wanted. I didn't need the bottle much, either, because I breast-fed Kanye. But I appreciated the prize and was honored to have won.

The trip to Oklahoma City was the first of many. Over the next few years, Kanye and I traveled at least a couple of times each year—most frequently to Oklahoma City. But we also went to fun places, like Florida. Glenda, one of Kanye's two godmothers, and I took Kanye and her daughter, Alexis, to Orlando and Daytona Beach. Disney World was some of the most fun ever. I loved it as much as Kanye did. In fact, I've been there four times—only twice with Kanye. On one of the trips, we found a place where you could record your own music video. This was before the days of karaoke, but it was similar. Kanye performed a Stevie Wonder tune. God only knows where that tape is today.

Glenda and I rented a car and drove to SeaWorld. On the way Glenda and I spotted these really cute guys driving in the car next to ours. Before I could even gear up to say anything, Alexis stuck her little head out of the back window and, pointing to her mother, said, "She's married!" Glenda was faithful to her then husband, George (they're not together anymore), but Alexis was going to make sure nothing inappropriate happened that trip, not that it ever would. It's funny how kids are so protective and perceptive.

While in Disney, we went to one of those time-share presentations. We had no intentions of purchasing one, but they rolled out the red carpet for us, complete with Disney characters to greet us. They even offered two days of free lodging and breakfast with the Disney characters just for checking them out. There was no obligation and it was worth it all to see the smile on those kids' faces when Mickey and the whole crew came out to greet each kid personally at the breakfast.

I found it very important to expose my child to many things. Glenda and I were always finding places to take the kids—either out of town or right in Chicago. I wasn't rich, or even well off. I always kept a house because I was taught that owning your own home is something that you simply must do. Renting was not an option. I found that it was usually cheaper to own a home than to rent, anyway. And while I rarely denied Kanye anything, it wasn't because I had it like that. I was very clever in saving my money and finding ways to give him things and expose him to things without breaking our bank. Sometimes I would shuffle the bills to make sure he had something.

I didn't make much as a professor, believe it or not, so I sometimes worked two or three jobs. I believe you do what you have to do to have the kind of life you want to have. I don't talk much about my struggles because I don't think about it that way. I just did what I felt I needed to do for me and my child. I had a vision for how I wanted things done with him, so I proceeded to just push ahead and make it happen—no complaints, no feeling sorry for not having more money or more help. I just did it.

As our kids got older, Glenda and I increased their experiences. Every month we would take them to a different restaurant so they could experience different cuisines—Mexican,

Japanese, even French. The trouble was, Kanye always wanted a hamburger and French fries no matter where we were. He even asked for a hamburger at Benihana! He was not that impressed with the cooking at the table, except for the tricks the chef did with the utensils. He just wanted his hamburger. But at least he was exposed to something different. Today, he tries just about everything.

Another thing you do when you don't have much money is find "free" activities. One of my favorite "free" places to take Kanye was the Chicago Academy for the Arts. They offered art lessons for children on Saturdays. Kanye was a gifted artist and I was thrilled that we had someplace where he could get more training for no charge at all. I was surprised that he and Alexis were the only black kids in the class. They both took art lessons in Hyde Park, too. There were special classes on cartooning there. Since Kanye had already become interested in computer graphics and talked about going into animation, I thought this to be a golden opportunity to nurture his talent and see if he'd stick to it. He still draws today from time to time. I know that skill will be enormously helpful in his clothing designs soon to come. And it was nurtured for free, simply because I was active keeping him active.

Our trips within the city and beyond were incredibly educational. A lot of times, the hands-on experiences end up being a much more effective way for kids to learn rather than through some of the more traditional approaches. It makes children curious and enthusiastic about learning. Passive learning is often boring, a waste of time, and ultimately unfulfilling.

Once Kanye and I took a Greyhound bus once from Chicago to Oklahoma City. The bus made several stops along the way, and one was in St. Louis. I wanted Kanye to see the arch, which he had only seen in a photo in his geography book. I promised him we'd go there in person one day and see it up close. Our ride up and through the leaning arch in the little cars reminded me of a roller coaster. It was an exciting day that included a visit to the St. Louis Zoo. Kanye loved zoos and was fascinated by all the animals.

It was a good trip, except for the bus ride itself. That was grueling. We suffered through the entire trip, spending much of it on the very last seats—the only two left on the bus— which would not recline. Kanye was only six and did not seem to mind at all. But I vowed then that we'd never travel by bus again if the trip was more than two hours.

One of my favorite trips was our excursion to Washington, D.C. I wanted Kanye to see the White House and the Smithsonian Institute. We traced the steps of the March on Washington, and even put our feet in the pool. Washington, D.C., was the perfect field trip. We saw so many sites that Kanye was learning about in school. He was especially fascinated by the space museum. We would have seen more, but money ran out before the fun did. But we'd seen and done a lot.

Kanye and I traveled a bit when he was growing up. All that exposure was good, seeing people from different walks of life. But nothing compares to the experience of leaving the good old U-S-of-A and seeing what's really happening in other parts of the world. I was blessed to be able to do that myself and bring my son along with me on some of those trips. As a kid, I thought those kinds of excursions were for the superrich and for those who'd joined the military. Since I belonged to neither of those groups, I was content with the idea of traveling around the United States. From New York to California. Yes, that sounded about right. I never even imagined going places as far away as Moscow, Russia. I never dreamed I would see Bombay. I never thought it was possible for me to live in China—as Kanye and I did for a year. But seeing those places, and bringing slides and photos home for my son when he couldn't be there, was an education that you just couldn't find in a textbook.

My first trip outside the United States, except a one-day trip when I was twenty-one to Tijuana, Mexico, was to India. Kanye didn't go along on that trip. He was only three and both his father and I thought it best that he stay home.

Besides, I was part of the Fulbright Scholar Program, selected along with ten other educators for a nine-week research project. We went to study life in India, particularly life for women and children. Our first stop was Madras. I remember going outside after checking into our hotel, looking up at the moon, and thinking, "Wow, that's the same moon we see from ten thousand miles on the other side of the globe!" It was sobering and at the same time exciting.

My colleague and best friend, Brenda Cullen, had put together the trip and a very full itinerary. Working with two other professors who were natives of India, the plan was that we'd hit all the best spots. We would learn so much and meet so many interesting people and go to so many places. I'd never imagined a trip of this magnitude, much less my first real trip abroad.

The hotel was modest—so modest that I was greeted in my room by a lizard who obviously thought I was invading his home. Thankfully, I wasn't afraid of a little green lizard. But my roommate almost broke an ankle when she jumped on the bed to get away from it. She was carrying on, showing her "Western ways."

The next morning, we left our hotel extra early so that we could visit the Gandhi Museum in New Delhi. For some reason it had not been on the original itinerary, but I was extremely glad it was added. I have always admired Mahatma Gandhi and knew that Dr. Martin Luther King Jr. had learned a great deal from him about nonviolent protest.

Since we were educators, on a Fulbright scholarship at that, we were afforded the opportunity of meeting Indira Gandhi. As I shook her hand, I was humbled by her great work and reminded of the profound impact that Mahatma Gandhi had had on the world. These are stories I would tell Kanye later. And I would expose him to as many places and cultures as I possibly could.

In addition to Madras, we visited eight other cities, including one of my favorites, Bombay. Bombay reminded me so much of Chicago, with the city sprawled right alongside the massive waters. The Taj Mahal, a place I'd only seen in pictures, was mesmerizing both at sunrise and sunset. We'd purposely gone at both times of day to witness the rising and setting of the sun. No less impressive were the beaches of Mahabalipurum, where I spent my thirty-first birthday. It was amazing to wake up right on the beach. We slept in rooms that were outside, covered only with mosquito netting. Later that evening, there was a party. I had no idea there would be a huge cake for me, and even small gifts that my colleagues had gotten in town. After we'd eaten a meal fit for a queen, they sang "Happy Birthday" and we danced. When I awoke that morning from my mosquito-netted room, I was astonished to see the long stretches of white sand almost completely empty. Only two gentlemen were on the beach, and to my amazement, one was actually levitating.

We left Mahabalipurum a couple of days later and traveled to our next city. I was more interested in seeing the people, the way they lived or existed, at least. As we drove down the road it was not unusual to see places in the hills that had been carved out and made into dwellings. The spaces dug out of the dirt were about seven feet long, five feet high, and four feet deep and often housed a family of six. Along the way, we'd stop at little shops or a place to eat. At one of these shops we were approached by a young man carrying a child, who he held out to us, and begging for money. The child was ashy black and extremely emaciated. He looked like an infant but we were told he was three years old.

We gave him some money and went into the shop. By the time we came out, he was on the ground, hovering over his child, who lay dead on the street.

I shouldn't have been shocked, considering how he looked—skin and bones and ashy. I had seen other kids look like that throughout the town. It was a look of death that you just couldn't shake. I was deeply saddened. I had a three-year-old back at home, so it was a little too close for me. I still think of it today. I can still see that little lifeless body and want to cry. I remember thinking how blessed I was to not be living under those circumstances. I thanked God for giving me a healthy child, for giving me the means to keep him healthy.

There are children in America who are starving and malnourished, but nothing compared in America with the poverty I saw in India. The worst projects and the poorest neighborhoods of Chicago look like Pennsylvania Avenue in

D.C. compared to that. Then there was the contrast. Not more than a few miles away were temples encrusted with rubies and emeralds. I was aware of their customs and religious beliefs. But I still could not understand how temples could be filled with so many precious stones while just miles away children were dying of hunger.

The nine weeks in India went quickly and I couldn't wait to get back to my beautiful, healthy child. I made a detour, though, to Germany to visit my dear friend Ernie Faye and her husband, Kevin, who was stationed in Wiesbaden. I spent just a few days there, even checked out a wine fest in a nearby town. I still have the little glasses the wine was served in. There was so much free-flowing wine that if we hadn't been careful, we'd have been crawling home. I bought more souvenirs for family and friends, but most of my purchases were for Kanye. By this time I was consumed (even in the beautiful hills of Wiesbaden) by the thought of getting back home to my child. I missed him terribly.

I vowed I would never be away from my child that long again. So when I got an opportunity to spend a year in China, teaching English as part of an exchange program that Nanjing University in the People's Republic of China had with Chicago State University, I was going to turn it down.

But the chairperson of the English department, Dr. Jesse Green, made it clear that I could take Kanye with me. My main concern, besides all of the expenses being paid—and receiving my regular salary—was my son. I couldn't see leaving him for a month, let alone an entire year. And I didn't have to. It was an offer I couldn't refuse.

I knew very little about China except what I had read or

seen on television—which wasn't much at all. It wasn't even
on my list of places to visit. But intuitively I knew that living
in China for a year would be the opportunity of a lifetime.

I began studying the language some and preparing for the
journey. Soon Kanye and I were on the plane headed to China.
That seemed like the longest plane ride ever—but we finally
landed. We disembarked and followed the instructions I'd
been given. But the plane was early and the university officials
who were to meet us had not arrived. Everything was so foreign, of course—the people, the language, the signs, the customs. We waited for about forty-five minutes, not knowing
what to do. Then two professors and a student from Nanjing
University showed up to greet us. Our adventure began.

Our first taste of China was the traffic. There were bicycles everywhere. I learned later that only those employed by
the government drove private cars. It was understandable.
With the streets so jam-packed with bicycles, there would
have been no room for that many cars.

Kanye was ten, and one of the only foreign children who
had come to spend the entire year. He made a few friends
quickly. One of them was Diego, a Mexican boy about
Kanye's age who had already been there for half the year. His
parents both taught Spanish. About ten professors, or foreign
experts as we were called, had come from across the globe to
work in the foreign languages department there: I and several
other professors from the United States, Trevor from England,
Ellie from France, Larissa from Russia, Diego's parents from
Mexico, and a wonderful lady from Germany who lived in
the apartment right across the hall from us in the Foreign Experts Building on campus. The only other kid there was a little
French boy. He was quite a bit younger than Kanye and

Diego, and rather spoiled, everyone thought. He was happy only when he was right under his parents.

Within an hour after we arrived, Diego's parents consented to let him accompany us for dinner to the Jinling Hotel, which was a very nice Western-style hotel we often went to when we wanted American food. It's not that we wanted it that day, but it was recommended as an excellent place to have dinner, so we decided to go there. Diego had already been in China for six months and had become pretty fluent in Chinese. He would be our interpreter for those first months until Kanye learned the language pretty well. I found Chinese to be very difficult, with its four tones and inflections that had to be pronounced just so. Kanye had fun with it. He thought it so amusing that the word "ma" pronounced one way meant "Mama." But the same word pronounced with a different inflection meant "horse." He played that to the hilt.

Every day in China brought a new and exciting experience. Within that first week I purchased a bike for both Kanye and myself, and we soon learned to navigate through the traffic with the best of them. It was our primary means of transportation, just like everyone else's. We'd ride for miles.

Kanye rode his bike to school every day, which was about six or eight blocks away from the campus. He was the only foreign kid in his class. Although he was ten, he'd been put in first grade because of the language barrier. I thought it would be awkward for him but he adjusted quickly. He learned math, some science, and especially the language, and for the most part got along well with the other kids. The teachers seemed to adore him. He was no doubt a novelty and the first black kid they'd seen in person. I was pretty annoyed that when the Chinese children would see Kanye, they'd yell,

"Break-dance, break-dance!" They didn't know much English if any at all, but they knew "break-dance." It was very stereotypical to me, but maybe the stereotype was based on the American culture as a whole, not just on Kanye being black. Still, I was annoyed.

It should not have surprised me to learn one day that Kanye had been putting his break-dancing skills to use. He could spin on his head and everything. Fearing he might break his neck or something, I always forbade him to do it. One day, as he approached me, I noticed he was eating a skewer of sheep meat. You could purchase it on the streets and we'd long since gotten over our hesitancy about eating the meat, which had not been refrigerated much less approved by the USDA. I had not given Kanye any money, though. I wondered how he'd bought the sheep meat. He'd been charging the kids to see him break-dance. I was amused and not altogether happy about it at the same time. I discouraged his little capitalistic venture, but I never really checked up to see if he continued. As long as he'd leave out the spinning-on-his-head part, I wasn't upset enough to put the fear of God in him about doing it. I never saw him with more skewers, though. Maybe he stopped.

Things were going pretty well. Usually the greatest of our worries was having to endure being stared down every time we went out. Not by just a few but by everybody. In China, staring is not rude and of course, neither Kanye nor I were regular scenery. Sometimes we didn't feel like being stared at so we didn't venture out. One time, though, we were in a small shop in the middle of Confucius Temple. In walked a group of Chinese, pointing and staring at Kanye. Before I knew it, Kanye had whirled around toward them and suddenly shouted *"gun hui qu,"* which in Chinese means "get back." Quicker than lightning, those people made their exit. Kanye, I'm sure, felt vindicated. He'd made them go away and stop staring, if only for a moment.

Even the loud command to "get back" paled in comparison to the incident that brought me to the school one day. Kanye had done the unthinkable. It was a cold winter day and in China, there was no heat in the classrooms, at least not south of a certain point. It was very cold in all the classrooms in grade school and on the college campus where I taught. Everyone wore a coat, hat, and gloves to try to keep warm.

Kanye had on all of that, but his gloves were the regular ones we had brought from the States. All the Chinese kids wore gloves with no fingers in them, I suppose so they could write better. Upon seeing that Kanye's gloves were not fingerless, his teacher approached Kanye to take his gloves. She probably said in Chinese, "You can't wear those gloves in here." Well, she did try to take the gloves but didn't quite get away with them. A tug-of-war ensued. Kanye was pulling on one end of the gloves and the teacher on the other. It was on, and the language barrier didn't help. Not being able to get the gloves from the teacher and put them back on his freezing hands, all of a sudden Kanye kicked the teacher and retrieved his gloves. I couldn't believe my ears when I heard what had happened. I was furious with Kanye. I had raised him never to kick anyone, much less a teacher or any elder. And yet it had happened.

Immediately the university arranged for an interpreter to accompany me to the school, and we all went trekking up the hill so that Kanye could apologize. When we got there, the teacher was waiting. She explained what had happened to the interpreter, who of course translated to me. I told Kanye how disappointed I was and that he must never do that again. Looking toward the floor, Kanye apologized. Then I explained to the teacher that while I would never condone Kanye's behavior, he would have to wear his gloves in the classroom. We could not risk frostbite in exchange for Chinese customs. He'd have to be allowed to wear regular gloves with the fingers in them on the bitter-cold days or he'd miss school on those days. It was settled. The teacher understood. Kanye wore his gloves from then on.

There was one last matter to address, however. "Kanye," I said. "You know you're to look at people when you're speaking to them. Eye contact is important. Why in the world would you look down at the floor?"

He then explained to me that to look at the teacher would have been rude and disrespectful. I had never realized that until that day.

The year in China was full of learning opportunities and outright fun. Kanye and I both became friends with the African students there who studied at one of three universities in the area, and learned to love the African cuisine. We went to many places in the city as well as around China. The Great Wall of China was one of them. Never was I so tired as when we climbed Yellow Mountain, though. That took a full day. I'd wanted to ride the cable car up and down, but Kanye insisted on the climb and I was too chicken to let him go with just my colleagues.

The mountain has lots of dangerous places, and if you're not careful, it could be the last mountain you'll climb. But we made it and got ready to take the drive back to Nanjing. It was a six-hour drive from Yellow Mountain to Nanjing on very bumpy roads. My legs were so swollen when we arrived back on campus that I couldn't walk and had to be carried to the apartment. In the end, it was worth it, bumpy roads, swollen legs, and all. Nothing was any more beautiful than Yellow Mountain.

At Christmastime, Glenda and Alexis came to visit. Lots of people said they would visit during the course of our being there, but the only ones who made it were Glenda and Alexis. The Chinese didn't celebrate the birth of Christ nor exchange gifts, of course, and Kanye and I were quite homesick. But when we picked up Glenda and Alexis from the airport, our whole demeanor changed. It was the four of us, along with my student Chang Don Bing, who traveled with us. She was also Kanye's sitter and language teacher, and was a lifesaver— booking tickets, getting cabs, and showing us the sites. It was more than an adventure and not easy. But Don Bing made it totally pleasurable and educational as well.

Once, Kanye and I literally took the slow boat from Canton to Hong Kong, where we'd spend two weeks before going on to visit Thailand. Around the Chinese New Year everybody went on a six-week holiday from the university; I'd decided on Hong Kong and Thailand, since Japan was much too expensive. In Hong Kong we stayed in what became known as Slum King Mansion. The bath was down the hall and the room was definitely no-frills. The cost was eleven U.S. dollars a night, if that tells you anything. But it's what I could afford and besides, who stays in the room while in Hong Kong?

When we got to Thailand we visited Bangkok first. Kanye went right along to the red-light district with me. I wanted to see it and I certainly was not going to leave him in the hotel with some sitter I hardly knew. From there it was on to Koi Samui. The beaches there are some of the most beautiful in the world. I was totally embarrassed, though, when one of the professors (also a Catholic priest) asked Kanye what was the favorite part of his holiday. Kanye answered, "The nude beaches in Thailand."

One of the many great things about being in China was that we could afford a lot of what we would not have been able to afford in the States. Kanye took tai chi lessons and got quite good at it. He also took private art lessons twice a week. He had private tutors in the evening, mainly Ezra, an African student from Zimbabwe, so that he would not be behind in his studies when we returned home. We would not have been able to afford any of this had we not been in China. Heck, I even got acupuncture every other day. Each treatment was $1.50. I'd lost my thyroid medication and thought acupuncture would work just as well, if not better. It did.

Without a doubt, living in China was a once-in-a-lifetime experience that neither of us will ever forget. I believe Kanye has forgotten all but one or two words of the language now. Languages are not like riding a bicycle: if you don't use it, you'll lose it. But I can envision us there on that campus and all about the city as though it were yesterday. I'm sure Kanye can as well.

We were on the go a lot from Chi-town to Shanghai and even took a ski trip or two in Wisconsin when both Kanye and Alexis were older. Glenda and I drank hot chocolate by the fireplace while they stayed on skis all day. It was just one more experience that contributed, I think, to well-roundedness.

If I had to point to any one thing that made a world of

difference in Kanye, I would point to his exposure through travel We didn't have a lot of money and were not able to see the world as he does now. But the exposure he did have was key in learning firsthand about different cultures and customs. When we didn't have money to do it up close and personal, we did it through books, museums, and eventually the Internet.

My hope is that more kids will have such experiences. I was lucky being a professor because there were a lot of travel perks. That's how we got from Chi-town to Shanghai.

7

L No!

There weren't many things that I denied Kanye. But there was one thing that I could not compromise on—his safety. He hates for me to tell this story, but I didn't allow him to ride the L train in Chicago. There were L stops all along the South Side of Chicago where we lived. I'd taken that train myself several times and caught it right at Ninety-fifth and State streets. Sometimes I'd catch it at Seventy-Ninth Street. But no matter where it stopped, I just wasn't comfortable with Kanye being on it when he was young. The neighborhoods weren't that bad to me, at least not on the surface. But dangerous things happened at those L stations and even right on the train.

When I first got to Chicago, Larry Lewis gave me a crash course in riding the L. He actually took me to the station at Ninety-fifth and gave me full instructions on boarding the train and getting from place to place. He knew it wasn't rocket science and thought of me as pretty clever. But he knew also that even with the few travels I had under my belt at that time, I might need a little assistance to feel comfortable on the L. Lots of people rode it: unskilled laborers, highly paid professionals, and everybody in between. Almost everybody seemed nice enough, but still there could be trouble, and frequently there was.

Larry was a native Chicagoan who had grown up on the west side of the city. He knew the city backward and forward and said I'd need to know how to get around on the L, just in case I couldn't or didn't want to take my car some days.

I appreciated that crash course. And it came in handy a couple of times. But recurring headlines in the Chicago newspapers about what had happened on the L was all I needed to decide that Kanye riding it, at least as a rule, was not happening.

Kanye wasn't particularly happy about that decision, but he didn't really object. As long as he could get from place to place by bus, with a friend, or by some means other than the L train, he was cool. But still, he was a teenager working on being a rapper. His music and image were very important. It was hard enough trying to break into rap being kind of preppy and from the suburbs. He didn't want to be perceived as being so spoiled that he couldn't ride the trains. That just was not cool. Whenever I'd begin to tell that story, Kanye would always stop me.

But I wouldn't let him ride them. People were getting killed over Starter jackets and gym shoes. The murder rate and gang activity in Chicago was no joke. We're not talking an isolated incident here. Not by a long shot. And I wasn't going to risk anyone taking Kanye's Air Jordans or his Starter jacket or worse yet, his life. Life itself was not sacred on the L, I preferred to drop him off and pick him up if need be. Otherwise, he didn't need to be there.

I hesitate to tell the story even now. I'm all too familiar with the press and the context they build around things. That was fifteen years ago and the next thing you know, we'll see a headline that says "Kanye's mama says L no." What I was really saying is "Safety above all else."

I was really blessed, though, because Kanye wasn't interested in hanging out and getting into trouble. He was too consumed with his music. There weren't any keyboards on the street corners, so he preferred to be in the house making music. He was comfortable there and I always allowed him not only to make music at home, but to have any and all of his friends over, too. At times it was nerve-wracking with all the noise. But I preferred a little discomfort to him being in the streets. At least I knew where he was. Besides, I couldn't overhear some important conversation I needed to hear if he and his friends were out on the streets.

Kanye didn't have a strict curfew once he got to high school. There wasn't really a need for one because he wasn't allowed to just hang out. It was fine if he was going to the park to play some basketball, to the mall, or to the movies with friends. But he needed to have a specific destination whenever he left the house.

I didn't like the idea of kids just chilling on the corners. I knew not all of them were selling drugs, probably not even most. But still it's easy for a group of boys to find trouble if they're just on the streets with nothing constructive to do. So we went a lot of places together, bowling, to the museum, shopping. And when he went out with his friends, I had to know where they were going.

When Kanye was growing up a television commercial aired for years that asked, "Do you know where your children are?" My answer was always yes. I felt it was important to know exactly where Kanye was or at least where he was supposed to be. I never understood why all parents didn't insist on knowing.

Was I being overprotective? I wouldn't say so. I was just being the best parent I knew how to be. I needed to know not only Kanye's friends, but the parents of his friends. That way, we could stay on top of things better. Besides carpooling to take the kids to school or a movie, we'd talk sometimes when they didn't even know it. We'd do a little collective parenting by comparing notes, and it helped keep our kids on the straight and narrow.

Most of that happened after we moved from South Shore Drive. After the bike incident.

One day while Kanye was out riding his bike in the park behind our house, some pretty tough kids, all older than he was, demanded that he give it to them. Kanye wasn't about to do that. Instead of handing it over, he jumped on it and rode off. As he took off though, one kid slashed the tire with a knife. I was through when Kanye told me about it. That could have been him they slashed. If it wasn't safe for him to ride his bike in a park that backed right up to our backyard, then it was time to move. I began looking for someplace else to live.

Call it black flight or whatever, I was ready to go. What if the next step was to recruit him for some gang or something? I wasn't having it.

It didn't take long to find the house in Blue Island. Scotty agreed to purchase the house and he, Kanye, and I moved in. I was still teaching at Chicago State and was able to arrange my schedule so that I'd usually be home when Kanye came from school. When I couldn't, Kanye came straight from school to my job at Chicago State until he was twelve. There he'd work on his homework until it was time for us to go home. It was a good arrangement. Kanye was usually able to complete most if not all of his homework in my office. That way he'd be able to watch some TV when he got in unless he'd used up his entire major network TV watching hours for the week. I restricted those and monitored the shows he did watch as best I could. I knew how damaging watching too much TV and watching the wrong kind of shows could be.

Public television was open season. As long as he'd finished his homework and chores, he could watch all of that he wanted. He knew what was expected of him, whether he'd sneak and break the TV watching rules while I was at work or not. Now twelve or thirteen, I'd be surprised if he did not...but Kanye knew what was expected of him and I'm certain that just having the rules in place, and being expected to follow them, made a difference.

I wasn't a drill sergeant, but Kanye knew if I expected something of him, he'd better comply. It was the least he could do. I worked very hard to make sure he had everything he needed and most of what he wanted. But he would be required to do his part. He would have to do his chores and follow all the rules. I didn't have that many but the ones I did have were important. No riding the L. No hanging out on corners. No watching too much TV.

Not talking back was another rule. I felt that was disrespectful and I still do. This didn't mean he couldn't disagree, raise questions, or express his feelings freely. I encouraged that. He just couldn't raise his voice at me or at any adult, that's all. And he never did (or almost never) because it wasn't allowed. I don't know what had gotten into him this one day though. I don't remember what the issue was. I just remember being startled that he flared up like he did. It caught me off guard but not so off guard that I didn't shut him down immediately. It didn't take hitting him. In fact my tone was quiet, deliberate, and very serious. Kanye was smart. He knew when I was serious. Just my telling him one time that I'd literally break his neck if he ever talked to me like that again stopped that behavior immediately.

I was indulgent, permissive, and maybe what some would consider overprotective. But I did not allow for one moment my son talking to me in a disrespectful tone.

Kanye knew also what I expected of him in school. He had to make good grades or else. That was his job just like mine was teaching. Since he was highly capable, there was just no excuse for him not to do well in school. I required that. From kindergarten through ninth grade he was an honor student. But in the tenth grade, things changed. Except for art and music, he didn't seem to care much about school.

I talked with him about it, like I talked with him about everything. There was no topic that was off limits, not even sex. When he was twelve, that conversation came up. It was my time to car pool and Kanye was in the car along with two of his friends. Jocelyn Elders came on the radio and as I remember it, she was talking about the rise of teenage pregnancy. That's when I told Kanye and his friends that masturbation was a far better alternative to having sex at such a young age. I told them it was perfectly healthy, normal, and gratifying and that they did not have to participate in sex with another partner and risk some young lady getting pregnant or contracting a venereal disease, not the least of which was AIDS. They said nothing. They just sat there anxious for us to get to school I'm sure so they could get out of that car.

I found out later my words had sunk in because Kanye told me so. But my words about the grades weren't so penetrating. Kanye's As were falling to Bs and the Bs to Cs. By the time he reached twelfth grade, I found myself telling Kanye, "Just graduate and don't bring home any grade lower than a C." But even that happened. He brought home a D in calculus and an F in French. I thought I would literally pass out. I was glad then, however, that I'd insisted on him attending public school—not that he would have had it any other way. But that allowed money for a tutor whereas private school would have taken every dime. We got a tutor soon after that report card came out and both grades came up: a C in calculus and a B in French.

Now if he could manage not to get suspended again or not to get Saturday detention again, we'd be home free. Thankfully, I didn't regard the infractions as too, too serious. Kanye's school had almost a zero tolerance policy, and he got suspended for going to sleep in Study Hall.

I stayed on Kanye though and he snapped back into what was acceptable. I was glad he did so I could resume indulging him. A few Cs remained, but I praised him for his accomplishments much more than I chastised him for his Cs. I was proud that he was winning every art competition that came along. He was also making million-dollar beats and I told him so. It wasn't just talk. They were really dope beats.

I tried to give Kanye the world as long as I thought he had earned it. Some parents do just the opposite. They are so strict that their children never get to find out who they are. They are so demanding that their children feel the weight of the world on their shoulders. I've never considered that effective parenting. Effective parenting requires being close to your children, which in turn requires mutual respect and balance.

I bought Kanye the things he wanted and he did what I asked of him, for the most part anyway. Admittedly, I was demanding, but now and then, I was not. Scotty on the other hand was a stern man who like me had high expectations of Kanye, at least in some ways. But unlike me, Scotty never let Kanye get away with anything. Sometimes it angered me. Kanye had to wash the dishes, mop the kitchen floor, make his bed, clean his room, clean the bathtub, take out the trash, and cut the lawn. And he had better do a good job at all of it. Even though I had my "no's," I thought Scotty was being a little too strict. But he was used to dealing with boys in his auto mechanics class and he'd had three sons of his own, all grown by then. I wanted Kanye to have the strong male input on a day-to-day basis, so sometimes I just swallowed it since Scotty was never physically or verbally abusive. Still, sometimes when Kanye wasn't around and couldn't hear me, I'd tell Scotty I wasn't raising Kanye to do manual labor. Nevertheless, I'm glad I didn't stop Scotty from enforcing the rules.

Children need the support and discipline of two loving parents, today more than ever. But we do not live in Utopia and it's not realistic to think that all children will have that. But we must do the best we can to provide experiences and set parameters that are most conducive to our children becoming happy, healthy, productive adults. Every child deserves that.

Some parents choose not to be as attentive as I was. Some might say it was a bit overbearing. But I disagree. You've got to set the no's, the boundaries early in a child's life. It may not be riding on the L that you object to. Your no's may be different depending on your own perspective. But parents have to "show up" as my friend Keith Cunningham always says. Showing up and being there is a prerequisite for accomplishing anything, especially raising a productive human being.

I'm glad I was both liberal and strict all at once. I'm glad Kanye was a good kid who understood and respected the no's. He was most times obedient and always respectful. That kept someone from having to get me out of jail for killing him. As I think about it, there were quite a few no's. But I am certain there were far more yeses. Parenting always has its challenges, and at times it is a struggle. But Kanye made raising him easy.

8

College Dropout

Kanye, can I talk to you for a minute?
Think you could probably do somethin' for the kids for graduation to sing?
—"Intro," *College Dropout*

He bought his first keyboard when he was fourteen. He had saved nearly five hundred dollars toward it. With the thousand dollars I gave him at Christmas, he had enough to purchase it. Maybe he knew then that it was music, not necessarily a college degree, that he was most interested in. I certainly didn't know that the keyboard would be his ticket out of college before graduation. I hadn't thought of a keyboard, or music period, as his path to success. Above all else, I certainly thought he'd get at least one degree.

Dropping out of college like he did was not my choice. I always emphasized education from the time Kanye was two years old. I thought education was the best way to succeed. I knew Bill Gates and others hadn't finished college if they went at all. But they were the exceptions. Besides,

I had that black, middle-class ethic that said you must go to school, do very well, and get at least one degree and probably more. I never heard anyone say, "Oh, I sure am mad I got this degree!"—even if they weren't using it.

Perhaps I wouldn't have been so eager to contribute to him buying that keyboard if I had known that it would ultimately lead to Kanye dropping out of college. But that would have also been the biggest mistake of my life. I had no idea at the time that he was so incredibly gifted, that he'd be able to cultivate and use that gift to acquire not only fame and fortune, but also true fulfillment. I knew he was good at art and music, but I never imagined him turning that into the career he has today. That was my limited thinking. If I had been thinking as big as he was, it would have been a no-brainer.

Four years in college or the opportunity to change the course of a whole genre of music and influence millions for the better in the process? Who knew that Kanye West would become Kanye West? Apparently he did. After years of my pounding the education mantra into his head, Kanye proved me wrong. I still believe in education. School is great and I still encourage it. The more degrees the merrier. But only if you're going to use them. "Use school, don't let school use you," is one of Kanye's favorite sayings.

Kanye has shown me the meaning of the phrase, "There's more than one way to skin a cat."

He purchased that keyboard and soon he was able to acquire turntables and a mixer. Later, he added a drum machine with money he made working odd jobs. He had an entire studio in his room (at least the basics), along with a bed, a television, and a pile of clothes on the floor.

Kanye dreamed of doing music from the time he was very young. I first noticed it when he was in third grade. That and drawing were his passions. But somewhere along the way, music took over. Kanye spent hours and hours mixing, rapping, and writing. It was nonstop. He became so involved that his socializing revolved around that studio in his room. When his grandparents Chick and Buddy would visit, Kanye would come out of his room only to eat and go to the bathroom. He was amazingly focused. If anyone, including my dad, wanted to spend time with Kanye, they'd have to go to his room and get in a few words while Kanye made music. Daddy did that a number of times. He was fond of being with his grandchildren, mainly to learn from them and teach them what they'd probably not learn from books. But if he was to teach Kanye anything besides what he taught him when we'd visit Oklahoma City at Christmas and for family reunions in the summers, he'd have to do so right in that bedroom studio where Kanye was preparing to be ready to drop out of college—if that's what it took to do his music.

There seemed to be a sound track playing perpetually in our home. It wasn't always pleasant for me. In fact, a lot of the time it was nerve-wracking. That thumping bass line seemed to shake the very foundation of our house. *Boom-boom-boom* day and night. All I have to do is close my eyes and think about it for a moment, and I can still hear that bass ringing in my ears.

By the time Kanye graduated from high school and had been out for a couple of years, I had had as much of the perpetual hip-hop right next to my bedroom as I could stand. I had listened to it for nearly ten years and even offered my sometimes solicited opinion on the tracks he made. It was

time for either his music or for him *and* his music to be somewhere else. Not that I was going to stop supporting his dream.
We'd just have to find another place for him to follow it.

I had considered turning my garage into a studio. I had
even looked into the cost of soundproofing it. But it wasn't
feasible. So the studio stayed in his room. There were all sorts
of people coming in and out of the house. And since my room
was before Kanye's, his music friends had to pass my room to
get to his. Most of the kids looked pretty wholesome—
hip-hop wholesome, that is. Mainly it was the thundering
bass that was no longer welcome—not all day and all night,
anyway.

I finally had to say to Kanye, "You're moving."

He was twenty years old and had announced that he
wanted to drop out of college. He'd use flattery to convince
me that his decision was a sound one. "After all," he said,
"I've had the professor in the house my entire life."

I'm now wondering if he came up with that line himself
or if Rhymefest, Mali, John-John, or one of his other very
clever friends had suggested he use that to win me over. Anyway, it worked—whoever came up with it. Yes, he did have
the professor in the house all his life. Now I supposed it was
time for me to see what he had learned that would bring him
success without a college degree. I had preached marching to
your own drummer and often didn't conform in my own life if
I thought there was a better way. But I'd come from a family
like so many other African-American families, where getting
your education was right next to believing in God. I'd even
put a little money aside so he could go away to college if he
wanted to—Florida A&M, Morehouse, I would have made

it work. But here he was dropping out of school to do beats. I was not happy. My plan for him included his getting at least one degree. But that was my plan, not his. I believed in him and I believed he would be successful with his music. But I never imagined my child not completing college.

Nevertheless, I was convinced that it wouldn't be the worst thing in the world—maybe next to the worst, but not the worst. I didn't really try hard to convince him to stay or say to him that he should have something to fall back on. From the time I was making my own decisions about what I'd major in and what profession I'd enter, I never thought of falling back. I was so convinced that the only option was to achieve whatever it was that I set out to do; it would be only natural if Kanye felt the same way. Never would I argue against having plan B. But once you're truly sure of what you want in life, if you're passionate about it as well as talented and persistent enough to go after it, perhaps it's better to spend that falling-back energy concentrating solely on getting what you want.

All the same, I was right next to devastated when Kanye first put out his feelers about dropping out of school. If he had said directly, "Mom, I'm dropping out," that would not have been the best approach and he knew it. It was much better to discuss it with me and bring me around to accepting the idea, although he probably knew for certain that he was going to do it when he first brought it up to me. Ultimately, I'm sure he knew I would support him whatever path he chose as long as it was positive. It just took a little time for me to really grab hold of the concept that college is not for everybody. Not for the Bill Gateses, the August Wilsons, or the Kanye Wests.

At least he'd tried college for a couple of years. He had gone to the American Academy of Art in downtown Chicago on a partial scholarship the first semester after he finished high school. It was very competitive to get scholarships and that he got even the partial scholarship for one semester made me very proud. The total cost per month without books, room and board, art supplies, or any of the other essentials was $1,100. I'd worked my way up from the $17,000 annual salary when I started at Chicago State when he was four, to somewhere in the $70,000 range. But the $550 I needed to pay each month for tuition along with the other expenses had me reaching back into that little nest egg I'd put away. Soon it would be depleted if he lived in downtown Chicago, stayed beyond the scholarship semester, and paid for everything else that was needed.

I didn't mind. If being an artist was what he wanted to do, I would gladly have doubled that $550 a month I had paid while he was on scholarship and sprung for the whole $1,100 a month the next semester. He stayed at home and the train fare from Tinley Park, where we lived at the time, was much less than the $1,400 a month they wanted for the tiny little space in the dorms. He went for one semester, then told me, "I don't want to be an artist." I knew then that although he went to his classes daily, had a portfolio that raised eyebrows, and really still loved the medium, he was much more interested in music.

"Fine," I said to myself, and then to him. "You can go to Chicago State University."

He'd still be in college, the tuition was already much cheaper, and I got a fifty percent discount as an employee. Chicago State it was. Kanye enrolled the very next semester.

He finished that semester and didn't do too badly. He'd become an English major partly because he liked words (or at least he liked writing raps with them), and partly because he didn't have to stand in the long lines to get registered. I was chair of the English department. It was nothing for me to select the required courses, fill out his registration form, and sign it. No big deal. As long as he showed up for the classes and did his work, I didn't really mind saving him the drudgery of a system that was a little less than efficient.

The second semester he was at Chicago State, his sophomore year, a couple of friends and colleagues reluctantly reported to me that Kanye was always either in the music rooms or the student union—not in the classroom. Walter, my good friend Dr. Joyce Joyce's husband, worked in student affairs and was the first to pull my coat. Then Kanye's English teacher confessed that she wished he'd not been in her class. He was very smart and a good writer. But he didn't always do his work, nor always come to class. Thinking it might help, I ran to the office of the English advisor, Al Brown, and asked him to talk with Kanye. Al was young and with it. All the students liked him. The girls loved him because he was so tall and good-looking. He'd actually been my student at Chicago State before graduating and going for a master's. I taught both Al and his twin sister, Alfreda.

He'd be perfect to speak to Kanye. Al would make him see the light. He tried all right, but Kanye wasn't really going for it. And Al, seeing Kanye's passion and his drive to do something other than get a degree in English, was wise enough to not really press the issue.

Desperate by this time to find ways to encourage Kanye to go to class and take advantage of this opportunity to earn at least one degree, I talked to several people. One of them was Robin Benny, the director of our composition program. I think she had a conversation or two with Kanye and saw that his alternative just might be a good one. I was surprised when she spoke to me on Kanye's behalf. Here she was, an educator just like me, encouraging me to realize that Kanye didn't necessarily have to complete college—at least not right then—to do something big in the world. She saw what I did not see at the time—a young man who had other ideas and expressed them very well, an artist with a passion who felt another path would serve him better.

I appreciated Robin's point of view, and technically, I even agreed with her. But it's one thing to agree with someone philosophically and quite another to feel good about the inevitable—your one and only child dropping out of school.

Well, it happened that semester, his third semester of college life. Kanye dropped out and never looked back. We made a deal. He'd have one year to make it happen. He would continue to live at home, but because he wasn't in college and pursuing what in my mind was the wisest plan, I would charge him two hundred dollars a month for rent. It wasn't that I needed the money. And it wasn't punishment for not going to school. I simply wanted to instill in Kanye the responsibilities that come with manhood. To me, if you'd finished high school and chosen not to go to college, then you'd chosen a path that brought with it financial responsibility. Kanye would need to earn enough money to pay that rent on time every month. That was part of showing me he could make it work.

He got a job working as a busboy in a Bob Evans restaurant. But when he reported for work, he decided immediately that bussing tables was not something that would work for him. He quit on his first day before he even started. It would have to be another kind of job for him. He'd never worked at McDonald's, Burger King, or any other food places. A restaurant was not going to work.

Kanye did have the gift of gab. So, he landed several jobs in telemarketing and did quite well at all of them. His first such job wasn't long-lived. One reason was that he was not allowed to doodle while he talked on the phone. But the main reason is that the supervisor insisted on pronouncing his name wrong. Kanye told her several times it was pronounced Konyay, with a long *a*. But she seemed to screw it up on purpose and would say, "Kanyee, Kanyah, whatever yo name is!" This angered him to no end. So one day, without even giving it a second thought, he decided to quit. I couldn't believe it.

His dad had bought him a new car. It was small and inexpensive, but new and sporty-looking just the same. He had to maintain it and put gas in it. My contribution was paying the insurance, and that was considerable for a male under the age of twenty-five who didn't have the best driving record in the world.

"Kanye," I said, halfway between calm and irate. "You'll have to go back in there and get that job back until you can find another." He didn't like that but he didn't really argue. And he even went back in and got his job back. Maybe he hadn't told them he was quitting, now that I think about it. But after another paycheck or two, he landed another telemarketing position. This one he liked much better. He could draw while he was on the phone and nobody cared as long as he was productive. He made a lot of sales, enough to even get a few bonus checks. He was so good that one day he called me and I swear I didn't even know it was Kanye. I just thought it was a telemarketer. I knew I had no interest in buying whatever was being sold. Actually, I hated those telemarketing calls. It was nothing to hang up on them. But since Kanye had become one of those telemarketers, I had started listening patiently and kindly declining whatever the offer was. Just as I was about to interrupt politely and tell the young man thanks but no thanks, Kanye told me it was him.

Kanye was making enough money to pay his rent and buy gas, fast food, and an outfit or two. But the problem was that Leonard, Warren, and a whole host of other kids (as I called them and still do) were trotting by my door nightly on their way to Kanye's room. If my door was open, they'd stick their heads in just as polite as could be and say with a smile, "Hello, Ms. West." They were all charmers, especially that Leonard. And I loved all the ones I knew. But that didn't make it any better. The bass was still booming and as I mentioned before, I had had enough—more than enough. That music and traffic were too much. They would all have to go.

"It's either you or your music," I told him. "You'll need to move out or find a studio away from the house. You can stay. But all of this music and these people have got to go."

"Mom, are you kicking me out?" He couldn't believe it.

But he knew I meant business. I rarely had to raise my voice or get the least bit ugly for Kanye to know when I was dead serious. And he also understood my point, totally. Well, wouldn't you know it, Kanye had been working with this young man called Gravity and Gravity landed a record deal.

He bought beats from Kanye to the tune of eight thousand dollars. I knew then that Kanye was going to make it. It's not that I had doubted it, but now I wouldn't just need to go on faith. Surely eight thousand dollars wasn't all the money in the world, or even enough to support him very long. It was the principle. I saw him making it work. It reminded me of when he'd had all his cousins in the mall in Oklahoma City one summer selling his first mixed tape. With their help, he'd made it work. And when he got that deal for eight thousand, I knew that millions weren't far behind.

Shortly after that, we found him an apartment in the Beverly section of Chicago. It was a spacious two-bedroom apartment over a dress shop. It had a huge living room and dining room and there was even a small room that he used for a studio. It was a perfect space for him.

The rent was a thousand dollars a month. The landlord was a little reluctant at first because Kanye was such a young man. I told the man that my son was very responsible and if there was any problem, I would be there to take care of it. I always pulled for Kanye. I would help him get anything he wanted. I certainly was going to pull for him if it meant getting that music out of my house.

He got the place. But the guy didn't like the traffic the music was attracting. It was in a commercial area and there was one other tenant, who was hardly there. She never really complained. The landlord just wanted Kanye out. That was his right, I suppose. It was his building. Besides, the lease would have ended sooner or later. And it probably worked out to be a blessing in disguise. It was perfect timing for Kanye to leave the city he had grown to love so much.

And I got evicted
packed all my shit up in a U-Haul.
——Kanye West,
"Last Call," *College Dropout*

Kanye, proud college dropout, decided he was going off to
the Big Apple, where it was all happening. Before deciding
on New York, though, he'd considered another hip-hop hot
spot—Atlanta. Jermaine Dupri was there and Kanye thought
perhaps he could find success there, too. He felt he had out-
grown Chicago. There was just nothing big enough popping
off for him there. It was his home, though. And I believe he
would have stayed if he could have made it big. So we went
to Atlanta, even found an apartment and put a down payment
on it. But New York was calling.

I had a friend, Richard Johnson, who lived in New Jersey.
We'd heard lots of people lived there and worked in New
York. It was settled. New Jersey would be a better (and more
affordable) place for Kanye to settle while he was trying to
take off in the music business. Richard found him this beautiful one-bedroom apartment in Newark, right across from Penn
Station. We rented it, sight unseen. It was $850 a month,
with a living room and a step-up great room with a glass ceil-
ing. You could actually look up and see the sky. It was wonderful. And Kanye was inspired. He said he knew he could
make good music there and I was pleased just as long as Kanye
was happy. The only thing that was not happening was the
carpet. A couple of cats had occupied the place before Kanye
got there and had not always made it to the litter pan. We
snatched that up and had Home Depot come and lay some new
carpet right away.

Kanye loved that place. He called up his friends and said, "Man, you should see this place. It's like something off of TV."

Kanye was exactly where he wanted to be. He was on his way to fulfilling his dream.

9

Rap or Bust!

Madison Square Garden. The biggest stage you can imagine, in the heart of New York City. Kanye could taste being on that stage. He could hear the crowds cheering, feel the adrenaline rush through his veins. He wanted to perform this night. He wanted to be on stage with the other rappers. He wanted to take this first step toward stardom.

But the answer was no.

Kanye had produced songs for the headliners of the evening—hit songs, multi-platinum songs. And all he wanted to do was be a part of it.

But the answer was no.

Instead, he was told he could have two tickets and watch the concert—a concert that some of his beats and songs were a hit in—from the crowd, just like everybody else. Two comp tickets, not even a backstage pass. He was very disappointed. What hurt the most, I'm sure, was that he knew in his heart that he could be a star—if only given the chance. But it didn't seem like anyone wanted to give him a chance.

Sure, they wanted him to make music, produce songs, and make beats. But they didn't want to let him rap. Fortunately, it wasn't up to "them." No one could stop him. Kanye had been planning this trek to stardom for far too long.

When he was just twelve or thirteen I caught him primping in the mirror one day. He turned and said, "Mom, look at me! I could be a teenage sex symbol!"

He was serious. It used to tickle me, him looking at himself in the mirror. It reminded me of my own brother, Porty, who used to look in the mirror all the time, talking about how fine he was. It was all in good fun. And very effective. Porty couldn't keep the girls away. And Kanye did become that sex symbol.

You have to be able to see yourself; you have to be able to see it when no one else can see it. You have to visualize where you want to be and claim it. Kanye claimed it a long time ago. But it didn't just come because he said so. Those countless hours in his room, the years of preparation and grooming for that moment, the work he put in, and the perseverance through all of the rejection, prepared him for when his vision finally came to fruition.

Sure enough, Kanye was going to be a star and a sex symbol. But that road leading there was a little more than rocky. There were a lot of closed doors and a lot of no's and a few dashed hopes before Kanye actually realized his dream.

The summer shortly after his nineteenth birthday, Kanye thought he had his big break. He was still in college and had no clue that he was even considering dropping out at this point to pursue music. When he told me he had a meeting in

New York with Sony I thought, "That's nice." But I still never put two and two together. I didn't realize that his "big break" would mean he wouldn't be finishing school.

Sony flew him out to New York and paid for all of the expenses. We didn't know that this was a customary practice when a record company had some interest in an artist. Kanye thought this meant he had it in the bag—especially when he saw the limo pick him up at the airport. He just knew he was in the big leagues. I could just see the driver standing outside of LaGuardia Airport with a sign that read: Kanye West. I just knew this would be it for him and I think Kanye felt the same way.

He met with several Sony executives, including Donnie Ienner, the president, and Michael Mauldin, who was head of Sony urban music at the time. During the meeting Kanye was asked, "What is your niche?" They wanted to know what Kanye planned to bring to the game that would be different. They wanted to know what would set him apart from the other rappers? Unfortunately, Kanye had no answer. He had never even thought about any of that. He just knew that he was good and was going to be the next teenage sex symbol. And that was good enough.

Well, it wasn't. And to add insult to injury, Kanye boldly predicted that he would be bigger than Jermaine Dupri. How was Kanye supposed to know that Michael Mauldin, the Sony executive sitting across from him, was Jermaine Dupri's father?! Needless to say, Kanye left there with no deal—and they didn't even supply him with a limo back to the airport.

When he got back home, Kanye did what he always did—went to work making more music. He was producing music and writing raps like the world was coming to an end.

But no matter how great his music was, no one wanted to give him a deal. He would soon learn that it would take more than talent, good looks, and desire to land a deal. He would have to add "resilience" to the mix.

If you're going to crumble when you hear the word "no," you can forget making it in the entertainment business—or any other business, for that matter. You have to develop tough skin. If they kick you down and bruise that ego, you have to brush yourself off and get right back up. And that's just what Kanye did.

He is like his grandfather (and his mother, too) in that regard. We will find a way or make one. That's just how it is. That's the difference, perhaps, in being a winner or a loser in life. Winners find a way. Losers don't. Losers wimp out. Losers have excuses.

There is no room in rap for losers. And Kanye certainly was not a loser. He's a winner and a worker. In fact, in his own way he's a hustler if there ever was one. He had to hustle just to get in and stay in the game. But his kind of hustling was different. He didn't sell or use drugs. He didn't join a gang, although he had friends in them. He didn't curse out the cops. But he did hustle. And he still does.

It was that hustle mentality and never-quit spirit that finally landed him his big break. It was the thing that Damon Dash, head of Roc-A-Fella Records, saw in Kanye and liked. It was what finally landed him that deal. Here was this young man being told no by everybody—Sony, Def Jam, Arista, Capital. And he kept coming. Somebody had to reward that kind of persistence.

We thought that reward would come much earlier than it did. Capital Records said they would be signing Kanye.

Joe 3H was unrelenting trying to get Kanye a deal and he called us and said that Kanye finally got one (or so we thought) with Capital. But before the ink could even get on the contract, there was another disappointment and another "no."

Kanye had been looking forward to finally signing with a label that believed in his talent not only as a producer, but also as a rapper. It went right down to the wire with Capital and I'm not sure what really happened but they pulled out of it at the last minute. Once again, Kanye had no choice but to bounce right back.

He took the rejection and kept working, and kept writing. Capital wouldn't sign him, but they did buy some of his beats for their artists. He played "Jesus Walks" for one of the labels. They wouldn't sign him, either, but they wanted to buy that beat for another artist. This time Kanye got to say no.

More disappointment would come before he finally made it, however. There was a Roc the Mic tour coming through Chicago. It was in his hometown, his backyard, and Kanye wanted so badly to perform in that show. In fact, he fully expected to go out onstage and do his thing, sing his verse on "We Are the Champions." After all, it was *his* verse. But once again, he was passed over. That was perhaps the biggest slap in his face.

He came to my house that night and I don't think I have ever seen him that disappointed. I don't remember seeing Kanye cry after the age of thirteen, but that night he looked like he wanted to. I was hurt for him. He was trying his best to take his music career to the next level but it seemed like there was always a block.

He thought this would be his chance to show what he could do, before his crowd—thousands of do or die, Chicago rap fans—on an open-air stage. This would be his chance to prove that Kanye West was not only a dope beat maker, but that he was a dope rapper, too.

He was backstage ready to walk out on the part of the song that he had rapped on for the CD, but the music shifted to something else right when his part was about to come on. It was no coincidence. It was just a blunt way of saying, "Not this time, dude."

Kanye was pretty down about it. But feeling down and letting people get you down are two different things. Kanye was on a mission and nothing or no one could stop him. Had he been another type of person, one who'd march to the beat of someone else's drum or one who'd listen to the naysayers, he might have left the rap game.

It was tough, as a mother, watching him experience rejection. I know he shielded me from most of it. I never knew about many of those doors closing on Kanye until much after the fact. As close as we were, he always wanted to bring home good news. I'm also sure that Kanye didn't want to tell me because it would give me more ammunition to get him to finish school.

But the rejection that I did get to see him go through actually made me support him even more. Seeing him work so hard and keep at it made me want it for him just as much. I saw his vision and I wanted it all for him—even if it meant him dropping out. It was important—for the industry and for me. Finally, there was a rapper whose words I actually could understand. Kanye's rhymes were meaningful and potentially life altering. He had to be heard. I would have done anything to support him. I was ready to wave a "Sign Kanye West, or Else!" flag, if I needed to.

Thank God, those rejections didn't stop Kanye or even slow him down. They seemed to make him even more determined. He never missed a beat (pun intended). He kept on making music in our home until he moved into his own apartment. He kept on making music there until it became apparent to him that he would have to leave Chicago to take his music to the next level. Kanye had met a lot of good people in Chicago—he even had the chance to be mentored by No I.D. and to work with Common. He was always at some venue in Chicago trying to be seen and heard, trying to break into the hip-hop game. But he outgrew Chicago. Like he said, "It just wasn't poppin' off like it should have been."

So he moved from Chicago. He chased his dream and caught it.

Kanye didn't get to do the Roc the Mic tour in Chicago. And he didn't get to perform at Madison Square Garden in New York City that night. He ended up turning down those two comp tickets that would have put him in the stands with the crowd. Instead, he went to the studio and worked on his music.

"Fuck that show!" he said. "Next year, I'll have my own show at Madison Square Garden!"

You have to speak things into creation. That very next year, Kanye West opened for Usher at Madison Square Garden. He performed a full forty-five minute set—on the same stage from which he was shunned. That next year, Kanye West had a record deal. Roc-A-Fella signed him, giving Kanye a $150,000 advance. He needed every penny. He used a hundred thousand to get out of the management deal he had and then had to pay the attorney, Londell McMillan, who got him out of it (he's the same attorney who got Prince out of his deal with Warner). With what was left over, I think he bought himself a watch from Jakob the Jeweler in Manhattan and bought a Mercedes SUV. He also bought me a Rolex for Christmas.

But it wasn't all about the money for Kanye. He wanted his chance to shine. And he got it. He was an artist. One year after all of that rejection, he was a rapper with a hit CD, *College Dropout*.

One year after being rejected, dissed and blocked, Kanye West was a major voice in hip-hop.

Through  the Wire: The Accident

I must gotta angel 'cause look how death missed his ass
Unbreakable, would you thought they called me Mr. Glass
—KANYE WEST, "Through the Wire," *College Dropout*

It was five in the morning when the phone rang, October 23, 2002. I picked it up and immediately recognized the voice. It was Sumeke, Kanye's girlfriend at the time. She was talking through tears, saying she hated to wake me so early in the morning, but Kanye had been in an accident. I sat straight up in the bed, fully awake at that moment. Before she could continue, I began firing questions. "Where was the accident? Who was driving? Was he hurt?" I asked her all in one sentence and in one breath.

"He's in Los Angeles still," she said, no calmer than when

she'd started. "I think he was driving. He says he's all right. But the car is totaled and they can't get him out of it."

I was stunned. Still, I managed to remain composed.

"Okay, okay," I said. "Calm down. It's going to be all right."

I asked her who had notified her and when she told me Kanye had dialed her from his cell phone and told her to call me, I was relieved. I knew that he would be all right, partly because I couldn't stand the thought of it being any other way and partly because he'd at least made the call himself.

"Sumeke, stay right by the phone," I said. "I'm going to try to reach him and I'll call you right back." She agreed and seemed just a little calmer. I hung up the phone and as fast as I could, I dialed his cell number.

"Hello," he answered on the first ring in a low, muffled voice I could hardly understand.

"Kanye, is that you, baby?"

"Uh-huh," he mumbled. "I was in an accident, Mom. I'm hurt."

My heart sank at the sound of his weakened, helpless voice.

"Kanye, where exactly are you? Do you know?"

"I'm not sure," he said. "Ma...Ma, I'm sorry. I'm sorry, I hurt myself."

Sorry? Hurt himself?

I had no idea what he was talking about and all I wanted to do was tell him that it would be all right. Before I got the chance, however, another voice came on the phone. It must have been the police or the paramedics.

"Ma'am, I'm sorry, but we'll call you when we get more

information," the man said abruptly. "I'm trying to cut your son out of his car!"

"But where is he?" I asked. "Where's my son? Where exactly is he right now?"

Hurriedly he told me where they were and that they didn't know yet what hospital they'd be taking Kanye to. He said he had to hang up. Kanye was still pinned in the car.

What?!

It was crazy. I was crazy inside. I had to get to my child immediately. He'd been in an accident and it was horrible and they were cutting him out of a car. I was also very calm. I have always been steady during a crisis. I somehow find strength and am able to gather my wits about me and handle the situation—no matter what it is.

I called Sumeke back and let her know I'd just spoken with Kanye and she'd better get packed immediately so we could get to him. I made reservations for the two of us to leave on the next flight out of Chicago to Los Angeles. My then eighty-seven-year-old parents were visiting me from Oklahoma City and were asleep in the next room. Mother had become very ill and had just come home from the hospital the day before. She, too, was very weak. What would I do about her? Without even thinking about it I called Helen, a very dear friend. I told her what had happened and she was at my house in what seemed like minutes. She told me not to worry about Mother and Daddy. She would be sure they were okay.

I called Glenda, who lived in Los Angeles. I told her that Kanye had been in a serious accident on Wilshire Boulevard and Santa Monica. Immediately she knew which hospital they'd probably take him to. She said she'd find out as much as she could and keep me posted. I finished throwing a few things in my suitcase, woke up Mother and Daddy and explained the situation to them, and headed out with Helen to pick up Sumeke and get to the airport.

By the time I got to the airport in Chicago, Glenda called with the news of what hospital Kanye had been taken to. She was on her way there.

I arrived in Los Angeles and for some crazy reason rented a car rather than taking a cab straight to the hospital. I guess I was just used to doing that and had not thought about the delay there might be in getting a car. It didn't take very long, though. I cut in front of the second person in line, explaining that my son had been injured and I needed to get to the hospital quickly. No one objected. I guess they could see in my face how serious I was.

Once I got the car, Sumeke and I jumped in and were on our way. I called Glenda and she guided me straight to Cedars-Sinai. I was on automatic. I had to get there and find out if Kanye was okay. In my spirit I knew he *would* be fine. After all, he had called right after the accident. If he had that much strength right after it happened, he had enough to pull through. Now was not the time for me to let go of my unshakable faith in God. I just kept praying. I'd been praying constantly since I got the call.

Oh God, let my baby be all right.

I probably made a string of promises, too, about what I would or would not do if He'd just let Kanye be all right.

I got to the hospital and Glenda was there to greet me. She gave me a big hug but didn't say much. She just told me where Kanye was and pointed the way. She seemed upset, but I was so focused on seeing Kanye that I didn't process it.

He was still in the emergency room. It had been more than eight hours since the accident and he had just gotten a treatment room minutes before I arrived. I guess he was just a regular black guy. He wasn't "Kanye West" at this point. He had just signed his deal with Roc-A-Fella. He had done "H to the Izzo" with Jay-Z, which was his first hit single. But his was not a household name—not that it should have mattered, because everyone should receive star treatment in the hospital.

I pulled back the curtain and there he was. Glenda had not prepared me for what I was seeing. I don't think anyone could have prepared me. Kanye was unrecognizable. Glenda had tried to wipe off most of the blood from his face and chest before I got there, but his head was three times its normal size. It was as big as the pillow they had it on. If I had not known I was looking at my own child, I would not have recognized him. His face was so swollen, so deformed. In fact, I thought perhaps it *wasn't* really Kanye I was looking at.

"Hi, Mom," he managed to say when he saw me come in. That was the only thing that confirmed for me that he was indeed my Kanye.

I couldn't believe he could even speak. But I refused to react. I knew he hadn't seen himself and I didn't want to alarm him. So I kept a poker face.

"Hey, baby," I said. "Oh, you're going to be just fine."

Right then, Glenda went out to the waiting room to get Sumeke. Only two visitors at a time could be in the little emergency room cubicle. I eased out for a minute with Glenda and told her to warn Sumeke that Kanye hardly looked like himself, so that she would not react. Then I came back in to see if I could do anything for my child other than just be there and try to share his pain somehow. I wished that I could have taken it for him. I thought about his career and about all of his plans and I wished it had been me in that accident instead. We'd not yet seen the doctor and I had no idea of whether Kanye's face would ever be the same as it had been.

I guess Glenda did a good job preparing Sumeke because when she walked in, she was pretty calm and collected.

"Hi, baby," she said. And then she hugged him. When she looked at his face and his swollen body, she told him, "It's not so bad."

It was horrible. But like me, she did not want to worry or upset him. Both of us could have gotten an Academy Award for our performance that day. In fact, we deserved a star on the sidewalk of Hollywood Boulevard. We knew, like everyone who knows Kanye, that he was very conscientious about his looks. He has always been that way. When he got braces, I remember his cousin Stephan asking him why.

"Because I'm going to be on TV," Kanye said. None of us thought he really needed braces. But Kanye wanted his teeth to be perfect.

Knowing him as I did, I didn't want him worried about how he looked, so I was going to keep up the front and keep the issue of his face out of the equation. Kanye would not be able to look in my eyes and see a hint of concern. That, I hoped, would be enough to comfort him.

His face was broken in three places. He had on his safety belt, thank God. But the airbag didn't deploy and his face hit the steering wheel with such force that it was crushed. Kanye, high off the excitement of his recording deal, had rented a Lexus, which is funny now that I think about it. His godsister's name is Alexis and so is his fiance's. Referring to neither of them, of course, in "All Falls Down," he wrote:

She's so precious with the peer pressure
Couldn't afford a car so she named her daughter Alexus (a Lexus)

Kanye was driving that Lexus at four in the morning and he fell asleep at the wheel. That's how it happened. When we were filling out the insurance claim, Kanye admitted to falling asleep. But one of the insurance brokers told him, "Don't say you fell asleep; say you were cut off or a car was coming and you swerved to get out of the way. If you say you fell asleep, you will be taking the next five years of your career paying off a negligence claim."

For several months we were riding with this lie. But Kanye called me one day and said, "You know what, Mom? I'm not lying anymore. I don't care if I have to pay millions and I'm down to my last dime, I'm telling the truth. I'll just make more money. Whatever it is, I'm just going to pay it."

I thought about trying to talk him out of it, but I knew that wasn't going to happen. I told him that I would handle it and he shouldn't worry about it. I told him to let me deal with the lawyers. But he was determined to make it right.

Kanye didn't just hurt himself in the accident. When he fell asleep, he veered into another lane and hit another car. The man in the other car ended up with two broken legs and was off work, unable to take care of his family.

"That man was lying in the hospital because of me," he said. "I have to tell the truth!"

Now, I consider myself honest, but I felt like a good lie could come in handy every now and then—especially against the system. Kanye was more highly evolved than I was in that way. He had been that way since he was little. He has always had a keen sense of right and righteousness.

There was this little Mexican boy in the neighborhood whose name was Tony. And people used to call him Tony Taco. So I said something about Tony Taco one day and Kanye got so mad at me.

"Ma, how could you say that?!" he said. "How would you like it if somebody called you Donda Chit'lin?"

He couldn't have been more than eleven or twelve, but that's the way he was. And that's the way he is to this day.

He didn't get that from me. If somebody broke into my house and stole a TV, I was the type of person who would say they stole two. I would justify it by saying to myself that they would depreciate that television and wouldn't pay me what it was worth. But it's still wrong. Kanye just was never that way. We had a flood one time and there was a receiver on the floor that got immersed in water. I told Kanye that we were putting that on the claim.

"Oh, no!" he said. "We can't put that on there. It didn't even work!"

Now, I'm not saying he was an angel. It's just that as a rule, lying was not his thing. Most times, even if he knew he was likely to get in trouble, ultimately he would tell the truth. So I wasn't surprised when his conscience got the best of him. Just one honest friend saying "Kanye, you should just tell the truth and be done with it" carried far more weight than any lawyer, insurance broker, or me justifying a lie that was weighing him down.

There was much to get through before he'd speak on the actual cause of the accident again. The pain, the swelling, the exams, the surgery, and ultimately the recovery were all-consuming. After the initial ordeal of being literally dropped on the ground when he first arrived at the hospital and was taken from the ambulance (he said that hurt worse than the accident), and waiting hours in emergency without treatment, there would be consultations and decisions that had to be made. What could be done about that face headed for Hollywood—or at least for a career in entertainment? Would the doctors be able to put him back together again? This was no fairy tale and he was not Humpty Dumpty.

When he whirled himself out of the bed all of a sudden and went to look in the mirror for the first time, he said, "I look like the Klumps!"

I was relieved to hear him joke about it. By that time, we'd seen the doctor, a world-class plastic surgeon, who assured us that through reconstructive plastic surgery, Kanye could be made to look almost exactly as he did before the accident. What a relief. I'll admit the doctor was also a pleasant distraction; he was very fine!

"My God," I thought. "Is he married?"

That was one good-looking man. So much so that it was the first thing I noticed. Of course, my first concern was his credentials, his qualifications to not only do a good job but the best job. But that did not stop me from thinking about how I could pull an Ivana Trump and go for someone who was much more than a decade my junior. Oh, if it had only been possible. Neither Billy Dee nor Denzel Washington had anything on this brother. Anyway...we were glad to hear the news and I came back to reality.

The day of the surgery, the whole L.A.-area family had gathered at the hospital. There must have been at least a dozen of us in the room. Sumeke and I were first joined by my sister Shirlie. She was visiting from Detroit and immediately summoned my nephew Little John to bring her to the hospital.

Big John, Deviett Jr., Jean, Yolanda, Lynn, Ricky, Corey, Sheila, Terrell, and Devietta all chipped in for the Thai food that would be somewhat of a comfort until the surgery was over. I didn't eat a bite. I couldn't. And after a while, several of us went to a waiting room closer to where the surgery was being performed and just waited. It's a wonder we weren't thrown out when we refused to leave the surgical area before we joined hands and prayed. My sister Shirlie led us in asking for God's mercy.

The doctor said the surgery would take only about two and a half hours. Nearing that fourth hour, I began to get pretty anxious. My cousin Jean was my rock. She held my hand and kept saying, "It's gonna be okay." I believed her but still I was nervous. Finally, the doctor came down the hall and we all jumped up when we saw him. Somehow, words would not come out of my mouth and it was Jean who asked the doctor how it had gone. He told us everything had gone okay, but because of some X-rays they needed but didn't have, it had taken a little longer than expected and further surgery might be needed. Then he quickly assured us that Kanye would be fine—he'd just be in a lot of pain for a while and his face would still be really swollen. We thanked him and God. I wanted some of that Thai food. But it was all gone.

The days went by fast and in another week or so Kanye was released from the hospital. We packed his things and headed straight for the W Hotel, where he was staying. Since he had to have medicine around the clock, I called my job and told them I would not be back until later. When? I didn't know.

The staff at the W was great. We moved into a two-bedroom suite and brought in everything we needed—a small refrigerator and a microwave. Kanye could eat almost nothing with his mouth wired shut. I spent a lot of time shopping in Ralph's, trying to find just the right juice, soup, broth, straws, smoothies—anything I thought he might be able to get through those wires. And we had to make sure he took that medicine like clockwork—every four hours night and day. I still have the medicine bottles and the little extra that he did not consume.

It wasn't long before Kanye was back at work—right in the W Hotel. That's where "Through the Wire" was written. He'd started it even before he left the hospital, thinking of the lyrics and rapping them through jaws wired shut. Kanye never writes his lyrics on paper. He just creates and remembers them, all of them, like a true genius. Sometimes I'd hear him on the phone talking as best he could about this dope song he was making and the beat he had in mind for it. Before I left, he convinced Roc-A-Fella to let him go back to the studio, supposedly, I believe, to make more beats for their "proven rappers." But in reality, he was making beats for himself.

Since third grade he'd written raps. By the time he got to seventh, he realized he'd need beats to rap over. That's how he came to be a producer. Now he was one. Painful as it must have been, he was determined to finish and record "Through the Wire."

The rest is history.

11

Jesus Walks

That means guns, sex, lies, video tapes
But if I talk about God, my record won't get played, huh?
—KANYE WEST, "Jesus Walks," *College Dropout*

I sat in the parking lot of Best Buy, popped in one of the ten copies of the *College Dropout* CD I had just purchased, and listened to all of it. I had heard snippets of the CD, even a few songs. But I had not heard the finished project. I had counted the days until February 10, 2004—the day the CD was to come out. I wanted to buy my son's very first CD—just like everybody else.

When I'd gotten to the checkout, at Best Buy, the cashier said, "Wow, you bought ten!"

"Yeah, this is my son's," I told him.

"No, it's not!" he said. "If Kanye West was your son, you wouldn't have to *buy* it."

I didn't have to buy it. I *wanted* to buy it. In fact, I came back a couple of days later and bought more. I wanted his first CD to hit the charts. I wanted the SoundScan numbers to go through the roof. I thought my meager purchase of just ten would make a difference. No way would I not be a part of the count.

I sat in that parking lot and listened to the whole CD. I couldn't pull off. I wanted to be still and take it all in. It had all of the skits on it. And Dee Ray was hilarious doing them. I sat there, listening—halfway holding back tears, halfway jamming. I had the music turned up real loud. I wanted to open my window and scream to everybody walking by, "Hey, this is my kid!"

I liked every song on the CD but one, "Home." That one just did not appeal to me. But all the rest of them were slamming. I was more than proud. I was beside myself. My five-foot-three-and-a-half-inch body stood ten feet tall that day.

It's hard to say which song I liked best, but one of my very favorites was "Jesus Walks." It had been almost a year in the making and I loved it long before it was actually finished. Two months before the CD dropped, the whole family was at home in Oklahoma City for Christmas. The cousins were all going to the mall as they always did just to kick it. But before they could leave, Kanye delayed everybody waiting on him in the car and asked my sister Shirlie to listen to "Jesus Walks." Shirlie has directed many church choirs and has been the director of music in lots of churches. She spent a lot of her life finding or developing talent, like Alfre Woodard and the Gap Band. She knew how to make people sound good whether they were acting, singing, or playing in a band, and Kanye knew it. He ran back into the house with the cut and popped it into the little CD player in my parents' house.

He started playing it. Shirlie was listening intently. Nobody dared say a word while she was listening. When it was over, all Kanye wanted to know was, "What do you think?"

She was visibly moved. She wasn't surprised that Kanye would write such an incredible song. But she was so proud that he had.

"Kanye, this is good," she said. "Reeeeal good!"

When Shirlie says something is real good, especially with such emphasis, it's like anybody else saying it's outstanding. She didn't have any suggestions that I can remember. Kanye thanked her for her feedback, and he and his cousins took off for the mall.

When I first heard the finished version of "Jesus Walks" on the CD, I was speechless. I was moved as much by the concept as I was by the lyrics and beat. Here was my child, right in the middle of a hip-hop album, talking about Jesus. I'm not a deeply religious person, but I am highly spiritual. I know people say that all the time. It's almost become a fad to be that way. But loving Jesus is no fad for me. It's a way of life. Being grateful is a way of life, too. If there is one word that describes how I felt at the moment I heard "Jesus Walks" in that car that day, it's "grateful."

I was grateful because Kanye was alive. His life had been spared in that terrible accident and so had everything else that enabled him, along with his friend Rhymefest, to write the song. I was also grateful because the song was so good in every way. You don't know if you want to dance or shout or do both when you listen to it. I was grateful because of the message many would hear just listening to the CD. I thought of the far-reaching impact it would surely have and became grateful all over again.

> God show me the way because the Devil
> trying to break me down

Here Kanye was not only open to it, but asking God to show him the way. Any doubts I had about hip-hop and Kanye's departure from college would now be gone forever. This dropout had dropped in to tell the whole world that Jesus walks. I knew that in thirty-one years of teaching, I had not impacted young people the way this single record would. It would also touch the old and everyone in between. To me, it was hip-hop and gospel, pop and blues all at the same time.

I didn't think about it in the car that day, but "Jesus Walks" would also bring many to Christ. Although there are many paths to right living, not just Christianity, following the teachings of Jesus is one of them. If people could be touched by "Jesus Walks" to the point of committing to a life of service, a life of helping others, what could be better?

Once when Kanye was on the road opening for Usher, he missed one of the concerts. I was not on the road with our team at the time and came all but undone when I heard the news. The crew had gone ahead, but Kanye had stayed back to visit with his dad and perform at a youth revival service his dad was involved in. He was to fly out the next morning, but the weather was too bad. Kanye hopped in a taxi without enough cash, but convinced the cab driver to take him nearly two hundred miles so that he could try to make the concert.

By the time he got there, Usher was onstage. Kanye was two hours late. He had missed his set and there were plenty of disappointed fans. But Usher, being the wonderful guy that he is, allowed Kanye to perform a couple of numbers anyway and I heard the crowd went wild. I was unhappy that Kanye was not on time for the concert. It was his ethical and contractual obligation. But I learned later that three hundred young people gave their lives to Christ the night Kanye did "Jesus Walks" at the youth revival. He was at the right place at the right time.

From the time Kanye was a small child, he believed in Jesus. He was raised that way. His father was much more religious than I and insisted that Kanye go to church every Sunday when he'd visit him in the summers. His grandparents on both sides were church going people and, more important, people who followed the teachings of Christ. I was also pretty adamant about Kanye attending Sunday school and church because I knew what a difference that had made in my life.

We'd go every Sunday to Christ Universal Temple in Chicago. I liked the church because the minister, Johnnie Coleman, preached prosperity. I had belonged to Hillside Church, which was very similar, before moving from Atlanta, and would take Kanye there. Barbara King, the minister there, was also a very spiritual and progressive thinker. I wanted Kanye to be steeped in that kind of exposure to God. I never bought into the fire-and-brimstone type of religion or one that was repressive. Certainly, I would not expose Kanye to that. But I felt compelled to see to it that a spiritual component was a key part of Kanye's upbringing.

I don't ever remember a Sunday that I did not go to church as a kid, except for the times I had the chicken pox and the measles. We didn't just go to church, we actively participated. It was fun, so I didn't mind it. My parents didn't just send us to church, they always took us. My parents were a part of our church—whether it was as Sunday school teacher, mission president, choir president, Baptist Training Union director, or trustee board member. I was not nearly so active in church once I was out on my own. But like my parents, I took Kanye to church. I didn't just send him. I wanted to teach through example and to do more than just send him off to Sunday school like he was sent off to kindergarten.

To me, a strong spiritual foundation is critical, and it was up to me to be certain that Kanye got that consistently. With a spiritual foundation, he would be able to do anything—even write songs that would win him Grammy Awards. It would be up to him how he wanted to feed that knowledge and develop his spiritual side.

Kanye, being so steeped in hip-hop, once said that hip-hop was his religion. Perhaps it still is. But he believes in a power that is greater than hip-hop. Kanye has always prayed. I'd hear him on the phone with his dad sometimes and they'd be praying. I'm sure that in many of Kanye's prayers he asked God to help him get on. He wanted a deal as badly as anyone could want anything. It was necessary to take the next step in his chosen career. He prayed to ask God's favor and he prayed to thank God for giving it to him. I know he still does.

Some may think it was the accident alone that inspired "Jesus Walks." I'm sure the accident, his upbringing, and every experience Kanye ever had factored into it. He was no stranger to spirituality. And I have thought since he was three years old that he had a special connection to God. We all do, but for some of us, it is perhaps more apparent.

He probably doesn't even remember this, but one day Kanye was playing in the dining room of our first home in Chicago, a third-floor apartment on the South Side. All of a sudden, he looked toward the door and the staircase leading down. He pointed and said, "Look, there goes Jesus!" My heart raced. I saw energy. To this day, I believe it was Christ giving us just a little extra protection that day. Neither Kanye nor I have spoken of it since. But it was very real to me and just one of the reasons I think Kanye is connected in a special way or for a special purpose. God has chosen him to not only reach but also touch millions.

Sitting in the parking lot that day, I didn't think about the Grammy potential of "Jesus Walks." So many other things were on my mind. I definitely didn't think about him performing the song at the Grammys. I definitely didn't expect to be a part of that performance. Late one evening, though, I got a call from Don C., Kanye's road manager. He told me that Kanye wanted me to play the part of myself in the production he'd be doing at the Grammys. There is a line in the song that says, "My mama used to say only Jesus can save us."

Now that I think about it, I was always saying something like that. I'd look at the devastation in the world and remark to Kanye, or even under my breath that God would be our only salvation. I never knew he was really listening. I didn't ever preach to Kanye that he must believe in God like I preached to him that he must wear condoms. I just lived my life thanking God for how he had provided. Kanye saw my unshakable faith and I guess he knew that it worked. To tell someone they must believe in God is not nearly as effective as believing in God yourself and having them see what results from your faith.

I told Don that I'd be at the rehearsal and do whatever it was that Kanye had in mind. When I got there, the choir was in the rehearsal room. The "Jesus Walks" treatment had been settled and it was hot. I was to be one of the choir members, doing all of the strategically choreographed moves. We were dressed in vintage church clothing—hats and all. We rocked that place. At the "mama" line, the camera zoomed in on me and I played my part like a true pro. I was no stranger to sing- ing, dancing, acting, or the stage. But to be a part of this was more than I could have dreamed.

Here was my son getting a Grammy and he'd asked that I be a part of it. Like many things since Kanye broke out as a star, this was surreal. When someone asked if I could get the part down in just one rehearsal, Kanye replied, "What?! You think my mama can't do what those church folks are doing? My mama can bust some Usher moves!"

I had no idea all that would come of that song when I first heard it. But as I sat there in that Best Buy parking lot hearing it for the first time, I knew it was very special—not just that song, but the entire CD. As I was listening to it, so much more was going through my mind. This was everything Kanye had worked for finally coming together. All of those years making beats and songs in his room. That thumping bass line that shook the house, all of those kids coming and going at all hours. It had paid off.

I knew it would. When I would pass by his room some- times, I would stop and tell him, "Kanye, that's a million dol- lars right there."

Listening to that CD took me back to those days; it took me back to the first time I knew Kanye was going to be big. It took me back to "Green Eggs and Ham," the first song I re- member of Kanye's. He was about twelve when he wrote it. We were living in Blue Island, Illinois, on Longwood Drive. He had a little group then and they'd practice faithfully at the house. Kanye would not be satisfied until we could get some-place to record that song.

Most of the studios charged by the hour and were pretty pricey. He had no connections and no reason for anyone to give him a break. The $125 an hour I was quoted was just not in the budget, not for "Green Eggs" at least. But Kanye would find a way. He was always finding a way or making one. He learned about some studio in the basement of somebody's house where you could record for $25 an hour. Twenty-five dollars an hour? It was a done deal. We were soon on our way to that studio.

The neighborhood was nice enough and the house was inviting. But when we walked into the basement so that Kanye could record, I saw why the price was so affordable. The arrangement was pretty makeshift, basic to say the least. But what I remember most was that the mic Kanye was to rap into was hanging from a wire clothes hanger, just sort of dan-gling there.

"What kind of studio is this?" I remember thinking to myself. But Kanye didn't mind. He was in producer's heaven. The recording session began and "Green Eggs and Ham" be-came a reality. It was the best twenty-five dollars ever spent, a precursor, no doubt, to "Jesus Walks" and so many other songs.

"Green Eggs and Ham" was clever and had a catchy beat. Most of all, it was Kanye's work and rarely did he produce anything that I didn't at least like, if not love. You know how mothers are. We put drawings on the refrigerator and leave them until they've turned yellow. They're more valuable to us than a Picasso.

But Kanye's work was akin to Picasso for me. I had been watching him do incredible things since he was old enough to talk. He was destined for greatness. Holding that CD with "Jesus Walks" on it, and everything else that makes it a classic, was a culmination of all of those years. My expectations and his had come to fruition.

1 2

The Roses

Coz with my family we know where home is
So instead of sending flowers we the roses...

—KANYE WEST, "Roses," *Late Registration*

None of the success Kanye has experienced would have been possible if not for the support of family. That support and love, as I mentioned in the first chapter, is just part of the fabric of who we are. We wrap our arms around one another during good times to celebrate and also in a crisis.

In 2004, we all got the call saying we should come to Oklahoma. Mother was deathly ill and doctors said that it could go either way. I'm sure they'd felt like saying "Get all affairs in order" and everything else doctors say to you when they don't think your loved one will make it. But they dared not say that to the Williams family, not about Lucille Williams.

She had been there before—close to leaving us. She'd had surgery nearly twenty years before after being diagnosed with cancer of the bladder. It looked bleak—bleak to the doctors, but not to us. We couldn't let it. For as long as Mother wanted to keep fighting, wanted to be here with us, loving and caring for us as only a mother like her could, we would fight right along with her.

She had been in and out of the hospital since the surgery in 1986, when she had undergone a twelve-hour procedure that, to this day, I don't know how she endured. We were there. We gathered together for prayer, as is customary when a family member is experiencing medical challenges. Shirlie, the oldest, would be the one to lead it. We bowed our heads and prayed with unshakable faith that mother would pull through. We did not believe in giving up, giving in to what the doctors said was probable. And sure enough, twelve hours later we were told she had made it. It would be touch and go, but she'd survived.

We all cheered like we were at a football game or something. We were screaming like we did when my brother, Port Jr., had stolen the ball and made the winning shot at Central High School's championship game. Teddy, his best friend, was much taller and was actually the star of the team. But it was Porty who had won the game.

But this was no game. This was mother's life. And we shouted, and cheered, and gave thanks. We knew that only by God's grace had she not succumbed to the cancer.

This time—twenty years later—it would be no different. The Roses had come from everywhere: Illinois, Florida, California, Alabama, even Canada. Of course, those who lived right there in Oklahoma were there, too. Some from Oklahoma City, some from Tulsa. How ironic that Mother was fighting for her life in the same hospital where she'd given birth to me.

I don't remember who showed up first. It was probably my dad, who knew all too well what those hallways looked like in St. Anthony's Hospital. But by the time that surgery was over, all of us had arrived, gathering in the waiting room on the eighth floor. It was filled to capacity, full of family, full of Roses who had come to make sure Chick would be okay.

Kanye was next to her bed when Mother opened her eyes.

"Hey, Chick," he said to her. "How're you feeling?"

Mother was weak but she mumbled something to him in a very low voice. We were all so glad that she could even say a word. Deviett Jr., my favorite cousin, was there from Los Angeles, too. He had flown in like most of us. But unlike us, it was his first plane trip. He'd been afraid to fly. Deviett is gone now. He passed in 2005, just seven months before my sister Klaye joined him in death, or in life. For me, it is only the physical body that dies, not the soul, not the spirit. And our Roses on the other side are still alive.

On that day we gathered to join forces in prayer, to support the matriarch of the Williams family. We didn't actually think of ourselves as Roses at the time. It was later that Kanye would describe the whole experience in a song and explain to the world that "instead of sending flowers/We the roses."

We didn't send flowers to his grandmother, who lay weak and was, some thought, near her last breath. Rather we made it by railway, bus, airplane, car, or any way we could. We ourselves came. As Kanye put it, *we* were the roses.

I don't know how the word spread that Chick was in the hospital and the doctors had actually told us not to be too hopeful. But I do know that in that hospital waiting room there was such a special connection among us that it inspired Kanye. He started right there in the waiting room. That's where the Auntie Team was formed:

> Aunt Shirlie, Aunt Beverly, Aunt Klaye, and Aunt Jean
> So many Aunties we could have an Auntie team.

The words are fitting. And all the players were champions.

Kanye's aunt Shirlie has always been very special to me and to our whole family. She was the first child born to my mother and father, and I'm sure there had never been two prouder parents. From the time I was little, I can remember seeing tons of pictures of her. They were everywhere. My father doted on her just as he did me when I came along. But she was the first.

More than a few times I've heard the story of how Daddy would make sure he'd sell more tickets by far than all the other parents so that Shirlie could win the title of Princess. Back then, there would be these fund-raisers at the school and the child bringing in the most money would win. Shirlie always won. She and my sister Klaye, who came along three years after Shirlie, were the first black children to appear on television in Oklahoma City. Klaye sang and Shirlie played the piano. Over the years, they sang and played all over the country. Shirlie still does.

Since Shirlie is fifteen years older than I, I really don't remember her living at home. She was brilliant and graduated two years early from high school. I do remember visiting her frequently, though. Shirlie had moved to Tulsa and was very politically involved. A militant Republican is how I'd describe her. Back then, many blacks were Republican, espe-

Kanye at the keyboard back in the day.

Kanye, Really Doe and GLC take a break from rapping. My dad had to step in to check 'em out.

Kanye's bedroom was a studio.
He spent more time mixing than sleeping

Kanye got his first keyboard when he was fourteen
and he never looked back.

Kanye in the kitchen with
rapper friends Shayla G and Timmy G.

Kanye in our
living room.
He was posing
even then.

"Look at my Gucci's!"
Kanye pointing to his
first pair of Gucci loafers.

My handsome son.

Kanye with my best friend Jahan, and Kaleem.
Jahan thought Kanye would grow up to be trouble.
Boy was she wrong.

Kanye moves to New York!
Okay, it was really
Newark, New Jersey, but
that was close enough.

Eric Dykes, me, and Glenda Lee at
my fiftieth birthday celebration—a black tie event.

Me with my sisters and brother:
Shirlie, Klaye, and Port, Jr.

My first Grammy party. Wow!
Kanye's godmother Glenda, his godsister, Alexis,
and I were all smiles. Kanye won three Grammys that night.

Me after
a hard workout.

Me and my superstar.

cially the progressive ones. I attribute some of Kanye's fire to his aunt Shirlie. He knows of her fire firsthand. She came to Chicago and lived with us briefly when Kanye was very young. Once, when she (and I, too, for that matter) had had enough of Kanye being late for the bus every single morning, she sent him out of the house half dressed, with his clothes, shoes, and socks in a brown paper bag, including his pants. She closed the door and told him he had better make that bus. Kanye went running across the street with his attire for the day in hand. He had to actually dress on the bus.

Fortunately, there were only a couple of kids on that bus because it was one of the first pickup stops. But Kanye got the message. I don't think he has ever forgotten that day. He was never late for the bus again.

Kanye was always fond of his aunt Klaye, too. She lived in Oklahoma City and went by to see to Mother and Daddy's needs every single day. He finally got around to calling her *aunt* Klaye after I'd said she was his aunt and he should refer to her accordingly. Before that, he'd just called her Klaye. She never minded. To her, Kanye could do no wrong. She was the one member of the family who didn't mind at all if he "peed on the white carpet." In the Williams family there are lots of sayings like that. When one can pee on the white carpet and nobody says a word, that means that person can do no wrong.

Klaye was around Kanye a lot during those early years. She had come to stay with us in Atlanta when Ray and I were still together. She was leaving a bad marriage, fleeing for her very life, she told me. I was so glad to have her stay with us, no matter the reason.

I adored my sister Klaye. She was petite and beautiful, a

jazz singer for much of her life. When I was young, she sang in all the local clubs in Oklahoma City. They called her "Little Miss Klaye, the steam heat girl." Of course, that was way before Kanye's time. But certainly he has that legacy. She was the first in our family to really make a living with her music. That she left that legacy is hugely important. But more important to me is what she told me one night when I was pregnant and feeling trepidation about whether I would be a good mother.

"Donda," she said. "I am here for you. Don't worry about anything when it comes to that baby. And if at any time you lose Ray's support, I will help you raise him."

When I think about her words, I still get emotional. Partly because they were so heartfelt when she said them, and partly because she is no longer here on this earth with me. Not physically, anyway. But I still feel her presence. I wonder if Kanye does, too. It is his aunt Klaye who told him there would be people who would try to bring him down.

"Don't let them!" she told him.

I don't think he ever will.

When my brother, Porty, was just twelve years old, he met the girl who would eventually be Kanye's aunt Beverly. We loved her from the very beginning. I certainly did. I thought she was much prettier, smarter, and nicer than Christine, another one of my brother's girlfriends who he was serious about. Beverly and Porty had met through my sister Shirlie at True Vine Baptist Church in Spencer, Oklahoma. That was a small, rural, mostly black town right outside Oklahoma City. Shirlie had taken both my brother and me to church with her. It might have been choir rehearsal. Shirlie played the piano there and Beverly sang in the junior choir.

According to Beverly, she spotted Porty when we first walked in and said to herself immediately, "I'm going to marry that boy! He's going to be my husband." I don't know how she could have been so certain that it would happen. But I'm sure that Kanye, for one, is glad. Every Christmas when we go home, Kanye stays with his aunt Beverly and uncle Port. She even makes an extra dish of her awesome banana pudding—a whole banana pudding just for him. You know the lyric where he says, "And that makes me want to get my advance out and move to Oklahoma and just live at my aunt's house"? It's his aunt Beverly he's speaking of. She's a godsend to us and to the entire family.

She was the one who promised my mother's sister, Aunt Ruth, who suffered from Alzheimer's disease, that she would never have to leave her home. Beverly went there every single day to see that she was well cared for. In those final days, Renee, Beverly's niece, took care of Aunt Ruth with tenderness like you've never seen, as did BeBe, Beverly's sister, Loretta, another niece, and her brother, Butch. Aunt Ruth died peacefully in 2005 in her bed at home. Beverly kept her promise.

Asked to retire early from Millwood Academy in Oklahoma City, where she'd put in thirty-plus years first as teacher, then counselor, and finally assistant principal, she did it. We needed her to come aboard as program director and executive secretary of the Kanye West Foundation, and if she hesitated, we never knew. She was never one to disappoint—only one to bring joy.

When I was just twelve years old and she was a freshman at Central State College in Edmond, Oklahoma, she invited me to spend homecoming weekend with her. I could scarcely believe the treat in store for me. A typical college student would have wanted to party and go to all of the places I certainly couldn't go. But not Beverly. She had invited me, her boyfriend's pesky little sister, on that very special occasion. We had so much fun that weekend. She showed me off to everyone and I felt as loved as I'm sure Kanye does each time he gets that whole banana pudding she makes just for him. She may be his aunt by marriage, but she is also his aunt from the heart and one of his very favorite Roses.

I believe that Kanye's aunt Jean, who is actually my first cousin and godsister, is the lifeblood of our family. She is perhaps the most fragrant of all of the Roses. My daddy's sister's only child, she grew up with us (mostly with my two older sisters, since I didn't come along until much later). If you could see how she loves family, how she showers each one of us with a love that we feel to the core, you would know why I call her our lifeblood. Of course Jean was there on that day "Roses" was inspired. If anyone was going to be there, she would be—all the way from California. My earliest recollections of Jean are some of my fondest memories. My cousin Deviett Jr. and I were about five years old, hardly old enough to tie our shoes. He always stuck his foot out for me to tie his shoe. I loved doing it. And I did it willingly until my aunt Ruby, Deviett's mother, insisted that I stop and let him tie his own.

Jean was crazy about both of us. She never minded having us around, although I'm sure that together we were a handful. We all lived in Oklahoma City, very close to my grandmother Williams, who we would visit almost every day. Jean would be there, too. It seems that daily she would send Deviett and me to the store around the corner, just about a block away, to get her a dill pickle and an RC Cola. She'd give us enough money to get her a whole pickle and a full bottle of pop, and one more pickle and pop that Deviett and I would share. I loved our daily excursions and I loved my cousin/sister Jean. I could feel even then, the special kind of love she had for family. There's something definitely special about the way she loves each one of us and how she shows that love. There's no way you can feel anything but uplifted when you're around her. She's going to see to that. Kanye knows she would do anything in the world for him. We all do. She's the most loving Rose of us all.

On that day when my mother, according to the doctors, wasn't supposed to make it but did, the hospital room got fuller as the day went on—not just with the Auntie Team but with all of us. At one point, we were pretty loud. That was right before the nurse came in and asked Kanye if he would sign some T-shirts.

Word had gotten around that the grandson of Mrs. Williams, the lady in room 805, was Kanye West and he was in the building. None of us would have been surprised if it had been Daddy who'd spread the word. There's not a prouder grandfather on the planet than Portwood Williams. He'd just as soon ask someone in the cafeteria, the gift shop, or even the restroom, "Do you know Kanye West?" Then say to them, "That's my grandson! You know his mother is a professor at Chicago University." He was always leaving out the "State" in Chicago State University. Not for any reason other than he just did. From the basement to the eighth floor and above, people knew that the Roses were in the house, and of course Kanye West was one of them.

There were many others. Port Jr. was there, my mother's

only son and the big brother I've always adored. You could never tell me as a kid that I didn't have the smartest, most talented, and definitely finest big brother of anyone. I even sold his senior picture for twenty-five cents a pop. It wasn't hard to do. All the girls loved him. Of course, my nieces, Yvette and Pamela, from Tulsa were there. They were always going to Oklahoma City to check on their grandparents. And they still do. Their older brother, Kevin, had made the trip from Tulsa with them, along with his daughter, Sharon—the oldest of my mother's great-grandchildren. Teandra, who now at ten stands taller than me and Antonio, the youngest Rose, was there, too.

Jalil, the actor/musician/gymnast/model and all-around everything grandkid, was there, as was his younger sister, Je-hireh, remarkably poised for a girl of ten and equally as beautiful. My nephew Don was there from Texas, as was my nephew Tony. Tracie, Tony's wife and Jalil and Jehireh's mother, also made the trip. No doubt she would make it. She always does. And we love her for it. Mike came, of course. He lives in the city, and with Sandy he'd always make his rounds. My nephews Stephan and Damien were definitely there. Wild horses couldn't have kept them in Canada. They never needed a special or serious occasion to show up to see Mother or Daddy. They'd come all the way from Windsor just to change a lightbulb if they were needed. Kim, or Cousin Kim ("Cousin Kim took off for work," Kanye shouted her out in "Roses"), came from Florida in a heartbeat. Eloise, Rosie B, and Joe Louis rounded out the clan. There on that eighth floor we stood, all twenty-six of us. The Roses were there in full bloom. And mother blossomed.

When I think about it, I fully believe it was the gathering

of the Roses that pulled Mother through. I believe it was our prayers and our presence that made the difference. We were her flowers while she lived. And even those who were not there physically gave fragrant and healing flowers through their prayers and through their spiritual presence.

From California to New York, Texas to Illinois, Maryland to Delaware, Alabama to Arizona, Michigan to New Jersey, the flowers came. And we formed one big bouquet.

There is nothing more important or more powerful. In that oneness, we can nurture and heal. Family members, biological or not, provide a foundation and a lifeline that is necessary for us to grow and thrive. It is important, critically important, to remain rooted. For what happens to a tree that is severed from its roots? What happens to a rose that is no longer watered, no longer nourished? It dries up like a raisin in the sun. Then shrivels and dies.

It was not only Chick who blossomed and came alive the day the Roses gathered, it was each of us.

1 3

Arrogance or Confidence?

If a hundred people who didn't know him personally were asked to describe Kanye, ninety of them might say that he is arrogant. In fact, that's the very first term that may come to their minds. Like the word association game: Kanye West? Arrogant! Not confident, not brave, not sure or certain. Not talented, witty, clever, or just willing to call it like he sees it. Just plain old arrogant. Some would say so with great adoration, others with outright disdain.

But for those who really know him, Kanye is anything but arrogant. He is mild-mannered, kind, gentle, sensitive, and always looking to improve himself and help others. That's how I'd describe him.

So what is the most fitting description?

When Kanye was just in kindergarten, his teacher said to me, "My, he doesn't have any problem with self-esteem, does he?" Readily I replied, "He does not."

But I wondered if there was a hidden meaning under her statement. I don't remember what prompted it. I just remember that I couldn't tell for certain whether she was complimenting him or indirectly describing a behavior to which she took exception.

Kanye was always a very self-assured kid. He knew what he wanted and how he wanted it. And he set out with great determination to get it. I never noticed him being willful in a way that was a negative or being insistently selfish to the detriment of others. But I did notice him, at a very young age, having what I thought was a pretty keen sense of self. And that's something that I always nurtured.

From the time Mrs. Murray, his kindergarten teacher, made her remark, and even before, I have known that what I view as high self-esteem, or at least the striving for it—a competitive spirit, a desire to win, and a lack of self-hate—might be viewed by others as arrogance, depending on who's doing the viewing.

Although we are constantly taught that it is a good thing to display strong self-worth and to stand and walk tall, we're often criticized when we really do that. We live in a world where we're taught to feel badly and get used to it. In some instances, the more we look down at our shoes and say "Yes, ma'am," or "Yes, sir," the more we are thought to be behaving appropriately. There is a contradiction in that somewhere. How are we to look up and look down all at once? Where do we draw the line between appropriately humble and sickeningly meek?

I'm familiar with the scripture that tells us the meek shall inherit the earth. But I'm convinced there is more than one way to interpret that scripture and more than one definition of meek. As I raise these questions and express my sentiments, it's probably clear that I am not one to encourage kids to wither away into the background, to be seen and not heard because it signals politeness. That's not how I would approach teaching any kid.

Of course, not everyone shares the same perspective on this. Not even couples married for years, like my mom and dad, have the same point of view. I can remember my mother and dad disagreeing about the then heavyweight champion of the world. Muhammad Ali was as bad as they came and my dad and I loved him. "Float like a butterfly, sting like a bee," he would say, or "Ain't I pretty? I'm so pretty!" We cheered him on, Daddy and I. But Mother couldn't stand it. She didn't like Ali and didn't really like the way my dad and I were always right there in his corner. She wanted Ali to win the fight, all right. But she could do without all that bragging. She felt Ali was arrogant and so full of himself that she scarcely wanted to hear a word he had to say.

Of course, Ali was not her grandson and she is totally different when it comes to Kanye. She adores him. And if she ever thought Kanye was arrogant—and she does not—she would probably just laugh and say, "Oh, that boy, listen to him!"

Arrogance to one person is simply not arrogance to another. If you say that you are the best and you really are, is that arrogance? If you say you are the best and you suck, is that arrogance? I suppose it depends on the tone and manner in which a statement like that is expressed. If you walk and talk cocky, putting down all others around, and display a nasty attitude in your pronouncement of greatness, then I'd call you arrogant. But that wasn't Muhammad Ali, nor is it Kanye.

All day long people run up to Kanye asking for autographs and wanting to take pictures of or with him. He can't even get a bite to eat in a public place without somebody, and often a lot of somebodies, coming over to get his signature. Celebrities are treated like gods and if they act like they've got the slightest sense of self-worth, they're arrogant. I believe if Kanye were truly arrogant, he'd have eaten a lot of baked potatoes by now while they were still hot instead of taking the time to graciously say hello and make some little kid, teenager, young adult, or even grandmother happy. Kanye is always so kind and accomodating. I'm not defending Kanye, because I don't feel he needs to be defended. I just want to set the record straight, to tell the truth about the issue.

It's not surprising to me that Kanye's persona makes people feel he is arrogant. Actually, as kind and considerate as Kanye is, even when he was a child, friends told me that I would need to put him in Boy Scouts. They'd say that there he'd learn to get along better with others. Frankly, I don't remember his not getting along with others, but maybe that was an issue. I do remember him wanting to have it *his* way. As long as he understood he could not always have his way, I didn't have a problem with him wanting to. He was taught to share and to be considerate. Granted, as an only child he had to share less frequently than kids in large families. But this is just the nature of being an only child. And being an only child in and of itself does not make one arrogant.

How can you say Kanye West doesn't work well with others? The nature of his business is collaboration. He couldn't have done what he did with Jay-Z if he didn't work well

with others. Nor could he have had successes with everyone
from Jon Brion and Alicia Keys to Jamie Foxx and John Legend to Chris Martin and John Mayer—and the list can go on.
You wouldn't want to work with someone who is arrogant
and difficult, would you? And Kanye keeps working.

I know his tirades and so-called tantrums can definitely be
considered a bit much. But whenever he has an outburst, I
believe it's with good cause. It's about making the best music,
the dopest movies and videos, the freshest clothes possible.
He's simply about being the best. Some regard that as arrogant.

Has Kanye ever behaved arrogantly? Absolutely! Not only
at a few awards shows, but at home as a kid. He went through
a phase at twelve years old where he seemed to care about no
one but himself. He'd think nothing of drinking the last Pepsi
in the refrigerator or eating the last of the cereal without so
much as a word to see if Scotty or I wanted any. Kanye would
drink that last pop or eat the last of whatever it was with
such indignance that I had to pull his coattail pretty force-
fully. I finally sat him down and said, "Kanye, I love you, but
I don't like you. I don't like the way you're acting. I don't like
the way you have regard for no one in this house but yourself,
and you must stop it, now."

I went on telling him about himself until he was at the
point of tears. I had had it with Kanye. I did not like what I
was seeing. And I was intent on doing all I could to ensure his
growing up with a healthy regard for others. Kanye understood what I was saying and began changing immediately. I
had come down on him with the wrath of Khan and I'm sure
he thought twice each time he opened the refrigerator.

I will not deny that even today, Kanye acts arrogantly on

occasion. But to me, this occasional behavior is not character-istic. I recognize those occasions, but I don't think of him as an arrogant person because of them. At awards shows where he has voiced his strong opinion about not winning, he has sometimes expressed himself in ways that, to me, were questionable at best. I think this, as well as his one-liners and sometimes stinging sound bites, are what has caused many to think of Kanye as an all-around arrogant person. So much so that many times when people meet Kanye they are surprised, even amazed.

"You're not arrogant at all," they've often said.

What Kanye is is passionate—passionate about every-thing he cares about. And it is that passion that has brought fame, fortune, better, and best. Admittedly, his passion can lead to what some may see as trouble. But that passion is his lifeblood. Therefore, I encourage it, applaud it, and learn from it. Whatever mistakes he makes, I am certain that he learns from them. And learning from mistakes means growth.

Like me, Kanye was raised to speak the truth as he sees it, the raw truth. And it's that raw truth that allows him to pro-duce Grammy Award–winning hits and sell millions of CDs around the world. He shares his passion with other artists and helps to catapult their songs to the top of the charts. Kanye pours that same passion, truth, and vision into every-thing he does. I would no more suppress his passion, which sometimes leads to the so-called outbursts, than I would sup-press his ability to make music. To stifle the former is to threaten the latter.

Do I wish, however, that he would be a little less vocal on occasion? Yes, sometimes much less. But not usually—especially when he's speaking about injustice in this country.

Because he is always expressing the truth as he sees it and as he understands it at that moment. He has been raised to look through his own eyes, his own lens, considering the world and others in it but not mirroring their realities, not even mirroring mine or his dad's.

When I think about it, it is evident to me that Kanye was born to make a difference. And that requires stepping out of the little circles that the world might draw for him. That means coloring outside of the lines. Ultimately, if you yourself speak truthfully, rather than politically correctly, you may on occasion find yourself agreeing with Kanye. You may even spew out some of the same feelings with as much passion.

I'm the wrong person to ask for comments when it comes to Kanye's so-called outbursts. It's been said that I may even be partially to blame. Maybe there's some truth to that. I'm not certain. But I have always been a rebel. And right or wrong, I have always spoken my mind. I have always preached standing up for what you believe to be the truth. And that's what Kanye does. That's what his father did when he felt the need to express his truths.

Do I believe that every word out of Kanye's mouth is a universal truth or that he is correct each time he speaks? Absolutely not. It would be absurd to think so. In fact, we have differences of opinion more often than some might think. But that does not impact my supporting him fully. I don't sit around supporting Kanye because I think he is always correct. I support him because he is my son, doing positive things in the world. That he makes mistakes and says things with which I disagree is a given. Sometimes I strongly disagree. And when Kanye says or does something I think is wrong, I tell him so—usually immediately. I may not tell the world so, but Kanye knows when I am not pleased with something he has said or done. I think he still listens most of the time. I know, like all of us, he is still growing.

It's been said that Kanye is a creative genius. With that, I agree. It's evidenced in his music, designing, and directing. Of course, the world knows him best thus far for his music. But he pours his heart into everything he does. And with that passion I spoke of, he expresses himself in multiple ways. The same passion he has when he creates his music or draws a picture is the passion he has when he makes such statements as "George Bush doesn't care about black people" or "I should have won that award." It's passion. And I would never stymie that.

As for awards shows, I can totally understand Kanye's anger and frustration. There have been times when he was led to believe he'd won a particular award only to get there and not take it home. It would stand to reason that in such instances he may think of the show as a spectacle put on for ratings. I suspect that his disdain for whatever he thinks is not real or fair leads him on the spot to a mind-set of "I'm going to give them a show." The award is not based on record sales or excellence. It's all very political. In the case of the MTV European Music Awards, I firmly believe that Kanye had the video of the year. So when he went up on that stage and said what he said, I understood. That was not my proudest moment—not by far. But I understood.

Why sit there, smile, and applaud when you really feel like you were robbed. I hate false humility. I don't go for it. There's a lot to be said for being a *gracious* loser, but my philosophy has always been "Show me a *good* loser and I'll show you a loser." While it's prudent and appropriate to be silent sometimes—some things are indeed better left unsaid—being honest and open about how you feel is not all bad. I didn't like Kanye making the comments he did, I didn't applaud it, I didn't find it amusing. But I understood.

I can remember being so outraged at one of Kanye's losses that I could hardly contain myself. He was up for Best New Artist at the American Music Awards. He lost to Gretchen Wilson, who is an exceptional country singer. But there is no way she had had the impact on the music industry and on her genre that Kanye had on his. It's of no consequence, of course, but I had never even heard of her before she received that award.

When they made the announcement, I could hardly believe it. Kanye had just performed. After the show, when he went to do press, I went along with him and was as disappointed as he was. Admittedly, I wasn't quiet about it either.

I suppose if Kanye won and someone came up onstage and went off, I would have a problem with it. But if they really felt they were better than Kanye, I would honor their feelings. We're dealing with human emotions. Real, raw, honest human emotions.

The first time Kanye displayed his feelings over losing, he was seven years old. He was always participating in talent shows and contests and he performed in this one talent show as Stevie Wonder. He wore braids, sunglasses, and even walked like Stevie. Lip-synching to "I Just Called to Say I Love You," he felt he was the star of the show. He had practiced that song for weeks, getting it just right.

On the day of the performance, the person handling the music cut off the record before Kanye was finished. He hadn't gotten to his favorite part in the song, "No New Year's day . . ."

He stood there for a minute, dumbfounded. He wanted to finish his song. Finally, when it was apparent the music was not coming back on, he walked off the stage. He didn't win. Backstage, he was one upset young man. He couldn't believe that someone had the audacity to cut off his record before he was finished with his act.

"I wasn't done!" he kept saying over and over again on our drive home.

"I know, Kanye. It was a mistake. There will be another talent show next year," I told him.

"They didn't finish my song," he said. "I could have won!"

"You will win the next one," I said.

He eventually got over it. He came back the next year and won. In fact, he won every year after that until the talent competition became just a talent show, so no one would have to lose. I liked his spirit after he'd lost, though. He didn't let a little adversity get him down. He used it as fuel to come back even better.

Everyone knows Kanye is pretty unhappy when he feels he's lost unjustly. And despite my disappointment in his not winning sometimes, I'll admit it may serve him better in the long run to be a more gracious loser—even when he feels he's been robbed. However, he will use that experience to do something even greater. Kanye hates to lose. He hates coming in second. It's just the way he's wired.

As his mother, I support him without exception because he will learn from the experience. It will help him grow as a person, and in the end he will find a way to overcome it.

That's what separates success from failure—the ability to overcome adversity and use that adversity to become even stronger.

All of this I say in the context of asking the question "Is it arrogance or confidence we see in a determined, strong-willed, expressive Kanye?"

Despite the opinions of others, I say that it is confidence. It's the confidence you develop when you're challenged or challenge yourself to be the best.

I always set high expectations for Kanye. It wasn't something I had to talk to him about. It was just understood. And it wasn't the kind of pressure that some parents put on their children, where the kids want to jump off a building for getting a B. I think that's unhealthy.

I never put any expectation on Kanye that I didn't believe he could meet and exceed. It was always clear that he could be anything he wanted to, so I wanted to make sure that he never had any excuses for why he didn't accomplish something. Exposure, support, encouragement, feedback, praise, and spending lots of quality time with Kanye have resulted, I believe, not in an arrogant person but a confident one—one who believes in himself enormously.

To believe in himself, however, meant he had to know who he was. Otherwise he might believe in some pseudo self, some figment of his imagination. So I made it a point to address the issue consciously. As an educator, I always posed this question to my students: Who are you? Naturally, I posed it to my own son. I was first confronted with the question myself in the essay "Who Am I" by Marya Mannes. I taught it for nearly thirty years in all my freshman writing classes and used it in parenting Kanye too. It raised one of the most important questions we can ever ask, the question of who we are. I don't remember the opening paragraph precisely, but it went something like this:

"Who are you? Not you together, but you singularly? When did it begin—that long day's journey into self? When did you begin to know that you are unique, separate, alone? We came from somewhere. Not from just the seeds of our fathers and the wombs of our mothers—but from a long line of forefathers before us. The time of self-discovery is different for everybody. Some, very few, find themselves early in life. For others the discovery comes later. But for most, and those are the tragic ones, self-discovery never comes."

This poignant message, though not offered here verbatim, is nonetheless one of the most important we can ponder. The essay continues to challenge us to think on the question of who we are. I believe all parents should ask their children this question at some point. I asked this question of Kanye when he was twelve. I did not want him to be one of the tragic ones. He answered loud and clear, not in words but through his actions.

I didn't sit down and tell him, "You have to be the best." I just always thought he was. This, I believe, bolstered his confidence and his enthusiasm in all that he did. And given how competitive he was by nature and how determined, it all worked out. I saw it in him when at seven months old, he was determined to get out of his crib and be free, even if he split his head in the process—which he did. That never stopped him. And he has been fighting to do exactly what he wants to do ever since. I suspect he always will.

Is Kanye the arrogant artist some think him to be? Well, arrogance is in the eye of the beholder.

1 4

Pink Polos and Backpacks

I don't know how many times I said it. "Kanye, pull up those pants!" It must have been a thousand. I finally gave up. He would say, "But, mom, it's the style."

I don't know how the pants didn't end up around the ankles. It was a physics marvel how they would hang just low enough to still stay on. All the kids were dressing like that. I wondered what would happen if they were chased and had to break out into a run. But if you were cool, that's the way you wore your pants. And Kanye was no exception. At least not at first.

He was around fifteen years old when he started wearing them that way. That's when Scotty and I separated and Kanye and I moved to Tinley Park. Scotty wouldn't have allowed him to wear his pants like that, not for one minute. I didn't want to allow it either. But after a while, you learn to pick your battles. As long as his pants didn't actually fall down around his ankles, and as long as the other rules I'd set were followed, I wouldn't complain. We compromised. He could wear them low, but not as low as I'd seen some of his friends wear theirs. They could hardly walk without their pants falling completely down.

I just couldn't understand this latest trend. It seemed ridiculous. And Kanye had all kinds of excuses for why the low pants were necessary.

"I have a big butt, Mom," he'd say. "I have to wear my pants low like this so it won't look so big."

But the day did come, thank goodness, that Kanye decided to have his own style. He stopped wearing his pants low and he stopped wearing those XXXL shirts that swallowed him.

I bought all of Kanye's clothes until he got into the fourth grade. And he didn't seem to mind. When I look back at some of the pictures of him in those early days, it's apparent that both of us were thinking about something other than fashion. Still, I thought he looked pretty cute in the clothes I bought for him. I especially liked the little Miami Dolphins letterman jacket I'd gotten him when he was two. He looked good in pastel colors even then. They were pastel, but still rich and didn't look feminine at all. That Dolphin turquoise blue and orange really popped on Kanye. I'd have him in that jacket all the time. It looked good with his blue jeans and Hush Puppies.

But some of the pictures tell a different story. The blue and red sweater that I put with brown corduroys when Tony, my then boyfriend, took us to the auto show at McCormick Place could hardly be considered fashionable. That outfit was sinful and I have pictures to prove it. It looked like something

I'd gotten from Goodwill. Maybe we were just in a hurry that day. Then again, it's quite possible that I had gotten it from some used clothing store. Quiet as it's kept, I loved a bargain. I didn't frequent the Goodwill stores, but I did hit the Uniques more than a few times. I used to go on Monday nights when everything was half price. I loved shopping where everything in the store was affordable. I'd gather up a whole basket of stuff that might only get worn once after I got it home. Regardless, my bill would usually come to no more than forty bucks. I thought that was far better than going to the local Kmart and buying half the stuff for twice the price, not to mention the quality issue.

I dragged Kanye with me a couple of times and he hated it. It didn't matter, though—not when he was a little kid. I was the one forking over the dough on a teacher's salary. And at five, six, and seven years old, who cared if the clothes came from Macy's or Second Time Around? After he got bigger and headed into those preteen years, any shopping I did at thrift stores was for me only. Being a typical kid, Kanye wanted his clothes to be new, and he wanted name brands. I'll never forget the day he was ducking around the aisles in Payless because he thought someone might see him.

I guess I was partly to blame for his name-brand jones. I bought him his first pair of Air Jordans when he was ten. What boy didn't love Michael Jordan then? And to have a pair of those sixty-five-dollar Jordans was something special. I'd gotten them in Hyde Park at a shoe store that specialized in shoes for kids. They had all the latest styles and brands— PF Flyers, Keds, Converse, you name it. But nothing could compare to the Air Jordans. Nothing.

Back then, sixty-five dollars was quite a bit to pay for a

pair of kid's sneakers. Even today, that's a pretty penny for a pair of sneakers that a kid will outgrow in a couple of months. But I didn't think twice about it. I would save in other ways, on other things, so that when there was something special to be purchased, I could once again borrow from Peter to pay Paul and purchase it. I didn't sacrifice getting Kanye books, or a computer, or anything else I thought more important than gym shoes. But he was a good boy. (Mischievous, but good). As long as he did what he was supposed to and earned his way, I was into getting him what he wanted, and he wanted those Jordans. I'd just have to find a way, that's all.

Kanye had wanted to be a fashion designer in fourth grade. But he still focused on drawing and writing raps. By the time Kanye was eleven or twelve, however, he'd become totally conscientious about how he dressed. That was when he first started doing his own laundry. One day he wanted to wear this particular outfit and it hadn't been washed. He was unhappy and I was not feeling it. I had a lot to do on a daily basis. I couldn't squeeze into my busy schedule making sure Kanye had a particular outfit clean on a particular day. He had clean clothes—even if it wasn't exactly what he wanted to wear. Now that he had become Mr. Style Guru, everything had to go his way? I didn't think so.

I remember clearly the day I told Kanye that if he wanted to have it like that, he needed to do his own laundry. That day, he started doing it, and he did it from then on. He became pretty good at washing and ironing his clothes. His grandfather, Buddy, even taught him how to iron his shirt collars and how to tie a tie.

I had given Kanye two hundred dollars for back-to-school clothes one summer and he came back with one pair of jeans and two shirts. I was outdone! He was in the eighth grade. With two hundred dollars I could have bought at least four pair of pants and four shirts, some matching socks, and maybe even a pair of shoes. But he came back with *one* pair of jeans and two shirts and thought that was okay. We typically shopped at Marshall's where you could get designer brands at discount prices. Kanye surely didn't shop at Marshall's that day.

I was so mad, I refused to give him any more money, not that there was any more to give. He was content, though, with those few pieces he bought. He was happier with those jeans and two shirts than he would have been with four times as much. That's when I knew he valued quality over quantity. And while I wasn't happy with him not getting more for the money I had given him, I begrudgingly respected his choice.

Initially, Kanye spent more time and had more interest in his art and music than he had in clothes. But once he discovered clothes, it was like a light went on inside of him and he poured the same kind of energy that he put into his art and music into putting outfits together and dressing well. It came without effort. When Kanye and his friends were preparing for a talent show or for some other event and they wanted "a look," Kanye would be the ringleader, in charge of deciding what that look would be.

At first, his style was to match. Everything had to match—black pants, black shirt, black jacket. That's what his group, Quadro Posse, wore when they won first place in the talent show at their school. The four of them did a dance routine and were all dressed alike—not identical—but alike in their black digs, right down to black shoes. The shoes had to be on point, too. That's one of Kanye's things. To this day, he is always telling me that the shoes complete an outfit.

"You can mess up a dope outfit with the shoes," he'll say.

Kanye became *my* stylist when he was fifteen. He'd critique whatever I was wearing whenever I had someplace to go. Sometimes he'd be kind. Other times, cruel. Once he even told me he'd give up his allowance if I'd go to Jenny Craig. I guess I was looking pretty fat in the dress I'd put on. I didn't get offended, though. I didn't even take it personally. And I did *not* go to Jenny Craig—not then, anyway.

Kanye always had some advice on how something or someone could look better. He's a visual person and always has been. He may be a little too frank on occasion, but he always wants to see people look their best, especially those he's close to.

Today, Kanye likes to be surrounded by people with style, people who know how to dress. I think Don C., Ibn, Leonard, John-John and all the rest of the crew would all have been fired by now if they didn't dress "fresh to death." If not, they would have certainly been teased to death. Poor Really Doe really hears it for wearing gym shoes that Kanye and most of the other guys think are weak.

When we're all together shopping, whether it's in Los Angeles or New York or even Japan, and someone sees a pair of gym shoes that don't quite cut it, we will say that they're Really Doe's.

"Really Doe left his shoes here!" someone will yell out.

I don't know where Really Doe (Warren) got his lack of taste in gym shoes, but he doesn't seem to be bothered by the teasing. He has thick skin. I catch it a lot, too sometimes. Just when I think I've picked out something that is really fresh, Kanye or Don C. or Ibn (John-John usually doesn't join in with them when it's about me) will bust out with the Really Doe crack. Or they may just shake their heads no.

Since Kanye is so into fashion, shopping is one of his favorite things to do. I'd say he's a shopaholic. It's habit now. Unless he's working day and night in the studio trying to meet a deadline for an album, he is going to get in some shopping. When he doesn't have the time to go himself, he'll send someone to pick up what he wants. Running around with Kanye and all the fellas in recent years, I'd begun to think that you need to have a lot of money to look good. But Kanye is the one who straightened me out on that.

Although he has money that is out of most leagues, he shows me examples of people who don't have a lot of money, but who look good all the time. They just know what they're doing when it comes to dressing. They know what looks good on them and how to wear it. I was glad he pointed that out to me so I can share it here with others.

You don't have to break the bank to look good! You can study fashion and go straight to Marshall's, or to the outlets and buy it for a lot less. This is not news to most, but it was to me. I'd shopped in Marshall's or some store like it since Kanye was a teenager and still wasn't getting it right. It's not the store you shop in. You can shop in Gucci and Louis Vuitton and still not have any style. It's not where you shop, it's what you buy and how you put your outfit together.

The trick, too, is not to buy just because something's on sale. If you don't love it or if it's weak, leave it on the shelf. That's common sense, I guess. But a lot of times I picked it up anyway because the sale was so good. That's one way to have a closet full of clothes you never wear or a style that definitely leaves something to be desired. I learned these tips from Kanye. And I must admit I get a lot of compliments on my outfits these days.

Fashion remains a big thing for Kanye. He loves it. He even brought his love of style to hip-hop. He wasn't going to look like every other rapper and he took a radical departure from typical hip-hop dress.

When Kanye first walked into Roc-A-Fella, everyone looked at him crazy because he wasn't wearing an oversized sports jersey. Even before *College Dropout*, Kanye was onto something entirely different when it came to clothes. The big jerseys with numbers gave way to sport jackets, and the baggy pants to a dope pair of YSL pants. When *College Dropout* dropped, people started copying, biting his preppy style—his pink Polo shirts, his proper-fitting khakis and jeans, his Louis Vuitton backpack. No rapper had stepped out of the box like that. Who would ever have thought it would work?

The sport jackets, the Polo shirts, and then the sunglasses made a statement. And the fans were loving it. Benae, the woman who braided my hair before I left Chicago, had a ten-year-old son, Akayade who was totally enamored by sport jackets because Kanye West wore them. One day, she ran across a Ralph Lauren jacket that was eighty percent off, with another discount at the counter. She grabbed that jacket as fast as she could. It was the perfect size, too. You have never seen a kid so thrilled as when he got that jacket. Imagine, a ten-year-old being thrilled about a sport jacket. He called it his Kanye West jacket. Every time he put it on it made him feel that much closer to Kanye West. If Benae had let him, Akayade would have worn that jacket every day—right over his Kanye West T-shirt.

Clothes that fit and that were by all standards considered preppy were not all that Kanye would bring to the rap fashion game. He brought the backpack, too. He became the Louis Vuitton don for the Louis backpack and other Louis apparel he wore. Some others may have done it before, but I guess that backpack, along with everything else—the preppy clothes, not being a former drug dealer, or gangbanger, or rapping about guns and killing—made it all stick. He was the definitive backpack rapper. He traded in green khaki canvas backpacks for the Gucci or Louis Vuitton ones and instead of filling them with college textbooks, he was filling them with his music.

Lots of mothers have told me about the impact Kanye has had on their children when it comes to fashion. They say the baggy pants worn low are starting to be worn closer to the waist. The huge, oversized jerseys are taking a backseat to the Polo and the polo-style shirts. Ralph Lauren (and others with a similar style) have sold more Polo shirts in the 'hood than he ever would have had Kanye not made Polo a household word. It's a new day in hip-hop—not just with beats that are more musical and lyrics that are more conscious, but with fresh-to-death clothes, too.

Now all eyes are on Kanye for his soon-to-be-launched clothing line: Pastelle. It's an upscale line for the highly discriminating and somewhat elite. It will sport nice colors (pastel shades, in fact), simple designs, and high quality. They are the kinds of clothes Kanye would wear and buy himself.

Remember the days when men couldn't wear pink? Now nothing's more fashionable even for some rappers than a stylish, pink Polo.

One of the hardest things for me now is what to buy Kanye. He's very particular and knows what he wants. Christmas 2005, I was beside myself trying to think of what to buy him. What do you get your kid when he either has everything he wants or could certainly get it? It's not about the money. Kanye always tells me to buy him something small.

Small or not, I wanted it to be special, something he would really like. Just as I was about to give up thinking about it and run into Best Buy to get the old faithful gift card (Kanye's a music and movie junkie so I couldn't go wrong with the gift card), Don C. and I just happened to talk. I was standing in the Louis Vuitton store waiting on my purchase when Don told me that Kanye had been talking about the millionaire sunglasses that Louis made. Hardly anyone had them yet.

"I can get them!" said Donna, the very cool lady who usually helps us when we shop at Louis Vuitton in Beverly Hills. And help me she did. She had them flown in from France and I surprised Kanye that year with those glasses. I almost broke the bank to do it but his reaction when I handed him those millionaire glasses was worth it. I can definitely see Kanye with a sunglasses line. I don't know of anything Kanye is as passionate about as he is his music and visuals, unless it's his clothes.

Was he raised that way? Well, it's certainly in his genes. My father is quite a fashion plate. He loves to look sharp. He's now in his nineties and he's still a sharp dresser. My dad likes to wear a nice suit and has tons of them. His wardrobe is full of stingy-brimmed hats and two-tone shoes—that's the way he always got down. Most of us in my family put a high value of dressing. And Kanye is no exception.

I'm glad that Kanye has a passion for clothes. When he looks good in what he's wearing, he feels good. But it's about much more than clothes. It's about balance. If you look great and have nothing else going on, what's the point? I was never bothered by what Kanye put on his body, as long as it came second to what he put in his mind.

15

Gay Bashing: "Yo, Stop It!"

"I think in the daily life of a black male, we gay-bash way more than we disrespect women. We would call a gay guy a fag to his face. But if we walked up to a woman and said Ai'ight, bitch! we would know that was disrespectful.

I remember five years ago I was in this clothing store in Greenwich Village with my old girlfriend. I said the word fag kind of loud and there were some gay dudes in the store. My girlfriend was like, "Yo, c'mon, step into the new millennium." Well, my level of consciousness has since been raised. And I actually think that standing up for gays was even more courageous than bad-mouthing the president.

In the black community someone could label you gay and bring your career down. But that was me showing what black people are really about today, or at least what we need to be about."

—KANYE WEST

I was always in the arts at church or at school, and it was not uncommon to encounter people who some felt were homosexual. In some cases, it was a known fact. But nobody said anything. It seemed that all the homosexuals were in the closet back then, except to one another, probably. Many of the male musicians were thought to be gay, and looking back now, a lot of them probably were. I also had a gym teacher in school who some said was a lesbian. She just looked athletic to me. Anyway, everyone commented behind their backs— but never maliciously. I never heard one person being outwardly persecuted for being gay. Perhaps that was because no one was out.

I could count at least ten people right now, probably more, who were known to be gay when I was growing up. Some were teachers at my high school. Some of them were choir directors, musicians, or ministers of music at my church or at other churches we'd visit. It was no big deal, and then again maybe it was and I just didn't know it. Maybe it was a big deal to those who were gay. They were the ones who had to tolerate the gay jokes and smile when inside they may have been bleeding. I'm sure that it must have been difficult at times not being able to be who they really were.

Many years later, I had a student tell me as much in an essay she had written on homosexuality. She was still in the closet and not happy about it. But she thought her family would disown her if she came out. She was glad to have a platform to speak. The experience had given her the courage to be who she was. To hell with anybody who didn't like it. But that was after I had grown up myself on the issue and opened my own closed mind.

Because of the silence on the issue around my house growing up, I learned to like the gay friends of the family a lot, and to fear the gays I did not know. Ignorance is not bliss; it's dangerous. So dangerous that I went off to college being afraid of any gay person who I'd not gotten to know in some other capacity before learning he or she was gay. How absurd.

My freshman year at college there was a girl on campus who was rumored to be a lesbian. I had seen her around campus but hadn't paid her much attention. I lived in a dormitory with about twenty on a floor, with a bathroom at the end of the hall that we all shared. I was hanging out one evening, heading back to my dorm room, and I really had to go to the bathroom. I ran down the hall and into the bathroom and there she was, washing her face or something. I didn't stick around to find out. I shot out of there and didn't even use the bathroom.

Looking back, I realize how silly I had been. Even if the rumor was true, what was she going to do to me? It's somehow assumed that all gays have on their minds is sex. Many never look at a gay person as an individual who has many dimensions other than sexuality. It's ludicrous, but that's how it is.

In the black community when I was coming up, being gay was something to be ashamed of. Labels helped to ensure that shame: queer, punk, funny. That's how people were described. I don't remember anyone coming out and saying, "I'm gay. Fuck off!" And I don't blame them. People had to go through so much just to be who they were—and some still do.

Growing up, I didn't understand the whole notion of homosexuality. When you come up in the church, you think it's some sort of disease that you can catch or cure with enough prayer. But as I began to broaden my horizons and really get to know people, I figured it out. Just as some people are heterosexual, some are homosexual. It's as simple as that.

One of the things that helped me see this was having people in my life who I loved dearly who happened to be gay. At first, I was like a white racist who has that one black friend but is unable to see that their black friend is not "special" or some sort of exception.

One friend of our family's, a brilliant artist and musician, is so close to us that he's considered family. It didn't matter to us that he was gay. He was always welcome in our home. You made exceptions to the rule. The rule being it's not good to be homosexual. But the reality was that there were so many good and wonderful human beings who were homosexual. And this family friend was one of them. He helped crush the myth for me.

I could list other examples. I won't, though, because the world is still cruel and I don't know how they'd feel about me discussing them in this book. Maybe they would say, "It's not nice to *out* Mother Nature."

I thank God that before Kanye was born I realized how absurd it is to be homophobic—how narrow it is to judge people on the basis of their sexuality. I wouldn't want to pass that narrowness on to him. But the anti-gay paradigm was deeply rooted in the minds of most Americans. Kanye was not able to escape it. It is so prevalent in the black community and is in most communities. Even as someone who always marched to the beat of his own drummer, he dissed gays big-time.

In hip-hop, defending someone's right to be gay was definitely frowned upon. You wouldn't think of expressing an opinion that was pro-gay. You'd better not even have such an opinion. It made much more sense to be antigay. And Kanye was. He wasn't just pretending to be. Like so many others—black, white, male, female, rich, poor—he thought homosexuality was totally inappropriate, maybe even repulsive. I'm not sure, but I believe he held these values not just for himself, a straight male, but for anybody else. Homosexuality was something to be hated, not defended, something to be scorned, not understood.

Besides genuinely feeling as he did, he was not going to put himself in a position to be further castigated. He wasn't hard. He came from a nice home and people considered him a mama's boy—the wrong ingredients for becoming a successful rapper.

I was never around when Kanye and his friends were gay bashing. But I can imagine the jokes, the attitudes, even the disdain they probably displayed. I don't know that any of them actually hated any gay person in particular. I think perhaps they just hated the whole idea. I believe a lot of young people are posturing when they gay bash. They are pretending to hate gays but really don't. Besides, how do you prove beyond a shadow of a doubt that you yourself aren't gay? By showing that you hate gays. The last thing you want to be associated with as a rapper is anything gay.

But Kanye came full circle the day he stepped up and called for his peers to stop the gay bashing. He distinguished himself once again not just as a talented rapper and incredible producer, but also as a courageous individual who thinks critically and is not afraid to speak his mind. Even if he is afraid, he does it anyway, which is what ultimately matters. Kanye made his comments in 2005. Looking back, he feels that that was "even crazier than bad-mouthing the president."

I'm glad Kanye realized there is no value in gay bashing. Nothing good will result from it. Even those who have a problem with homosexuality because they consider it to be immoral shouldn't cast stones. Isn't that just as immoral? People have lost their lives just because they were gay. They became "strange fruit hanging from a tree."

Until I heard Kanye speaking on it in interviews, I never knew he had disliked or ridiculed gays. My nephew, his first cousin and one of his favorites at that, would come over frequently. The whole family is crazy about him, always has been. He's a dynamic person who leads a very productive and successful life. What's not to love about him, his sexual preference? Give me a fucking break! There's stupid, more stupid, and most stupid. And to not love my nephew because of his sexuality would be the latter.

Kanye is none of those. In fact, he is the exact opposite. Ingenious. So I wasn't surprised when it dawned on him that despite the heat he might take by speaking out against the gay bashing—if indeed he even thought about that—he'd speak his mind.

Kanye's words were welcomed and applauded by many. Phone calls and mail came in to prove it. Heterosexuals, gay activists, closet gays, all voiced their approval via internet or some other medium. I was proud that Kanye had spoken up, that he had taken a stand. He's made a name for himself in hip-hop, won awards, and made millions of dollars. He could have just kept quiet and kept it moving. He could have played it safe. But he didn't.

This is my cousin. I love him and I've been discriminating against gays. It's not just hip-hop, but America just discriminates against gay people. I want to just come on TV, and just tell my rappers, just tell my friends, "Yo, stop it!"

—KANYE WEST, in an August 2005,

"All Eyes on Kanye West" MTV special

I hope everybody will stop it. Like comedian Wanda Sykes said about people protesting gay marriage, "If you don't like it, don't marry a gay person!"

Kanye's cousin has been out of the closet for more than fifteen years. He brings his partner home to Oklahoma City for Christmas and has for the last ten years. We love his partner. He, too, is an outstanding human being. It's cool that no one raises an eyebrow when I introduce them as my nephews, especially since my nephew's partner is white. Even my mother, who is ninety-plus years young, has a totally open mind about the relationship.

"We have people in *our* family who are gay," she once said. "It's not what you do, it's how you do it."

Everybody doesn't have the opportunity to explore their true selves in a family that won't judge them. That's a shame. It is a very weak person who downs others for being themselves. But in another context, I understand this. Sometimes you judge others when you're least happy with yourself. You look outward to find some deficit in someone else. It's not even conscious. I've done the same thing, although all my life I have prided myself on not being judgmental.

When Kanye spoke out against gay bashing, he didn't

show up to create a stir or to be controversial. He just felt like it was time to say something that needed to be said. It's doubtful that he thought very long about the risks involved, if he thought about that at all. He was too busy concentrating on what needed to be said—he thought more about the message than the messenger. He spoke eloquently and truthfully about something that was and still is critically important. When you have a platform and millions of people listening to you— not just hearing some words you utter because you happen to be on TV or in front of an interviewer for a widely circulated magazine—it's important to speak the truth as you see it. Crazy or not, it makes a lot of sense.

Thank God, we've seen a lot of breakthroughs over the past decade on the whole gay rights issue. In some places it has almost become popular, a fad, to be gay. Ang Lee won an Oscar for *Brokeback Mountain*. Television shows like *The L Word*, *Six Feet Under*, *Queer Eye for the Straight Guy*, and *Will and Grace* feature gay characters and affirm the gay lifestyle. Even soap operas like *All My Children* have had story lines that in some way embrace gay life. Sometimes those ways are as "out there" as it gets.

Well-respected people like Ellen DeGeneres, Rosie O'Donnell, and many others have had the courage to step up and say, "This is who I am." I admire and applaud them for being open and honest, but most of all for loving themselves.

If I could count the words Kanye has spoken that some people have found inappropriate, controversial, in poor taste, or just downright crazy, I would still be counting. But I'd bet you a year's salary that most of those words would be right on the money. "Yo, stop it!" are three of them.

16

Nigga vs. Nigger

That's that crack music, nigga
that real black music, nigga

—KANYE WEST,

"Crack Music," *Late Registration*

I grew up in the 1950s——the heart of the struggle for equality and humanity for blacks in America. My parents were activists in the movement. My whole family was involved—I was even arrested at the age of six for participating in a sit-in. Needless to say the word "nigger" wasn't welcome in my home. In fact, we couldn't say it anywhere unless we wanted to be in serious trouble. My siblings and I never even thought about saying the word. It was just understood that this word, "nigger," was offensive. It was right up there with "shit" and "damn," which we were off limits to us, too. But I think "nigger" was probably worse in my parents' eyes.

"Nigger" was associated with slavery and Jim Crow, lynchings and disrespect. It was the word that was used to downgrade and destroy blacks. It was the tool to humiliate and separate.

But even back then, when the there was so much tension around race, when that word nigger had so much power, there were still places in the black community where it was used. On occasion, I heard the grown-ups use it affectionately.

"You my nigga if you don't get no bigga, and if you get any bigga you'll be my bigga nigga," they'd say.

So I guess from the beginning there was some conflict over its use.

I do remember when it was used by blacks, that it had a different intonation. The word was pronounced differently. It was "nigga," not "nigger." It took on different meanings depending on who was saying it and the intent behind it. You could say it affectionately, vehemently, or indifferently.

"That nigga's crazy," might be said quite jovially. While, "I hate that nigga," took on a different tone altogether.

Nevertheless, because of the way I was brought up, and because of its use historically, I came to abhor the term. I reached a point where I never used it and never wanted to hear it used. I thought it played right into the white man's hands.

I felt obliged to hate the word "nigger." It was a strong feeling. I had heard the word nigger personally from the mouths of the most southern of whites. I thought of the Ku Klux Klan when I heard it and the treacherous acts they committed. And then there were Emmett Till and so many others who took their dying breaths with that word floating over them. As the years went on, I grew to hate the word even more than I had as a teenager and young adult. It was personal.

In the 1990s, there was a push to remove the word "nig-ger" from the dictionary. I was the chair of the English de-partment at Chicago State University at the time and was asked to speak before the Illinois State Legislature, which was holding hearings on the matter. I was adamant as I spoke about the damaging effects of the word and its association with everything bad and foul. I spoke about how that word was only applied to blacks and was detrimental to our psy-chological health. That word, I believed, should have been taken out of the language, period—end of story.

Ironically, having held that perspective about the word "nigger" almost all my life, today I am not bothered when black people use it, especially in the contexts in which I usu-ally hear black people using it. I know how it was used his-torically and how white racists and some blacks still use it today. But being aware of our history and conscious that rac-ism is still a huge problem in the world doesn't make me hate the word like I once did.

Although I'm still not always comfortable personally using the word, when I do hear it used in an endearing way, I don't question the motive or the consciousness of the person using it. And when I hear it used in any negative context, it doesn't sting the way it once did. Now don't get me wrong, I will *never* sanction white people or anybody other than blacks using the word. But when they do, it doesn't make me react the way it once did.

It's like somebody calling my mother a bitch. I wouldn't like it. But I know that my mother's not a bitch, so it wouldn't bother me. They can say it all day and it still will not make it true. So I don't give it any energy. I won't give the caller any power or credibility whatsoever. I know who my mother is and I know who I am. Calling me a nigger will never make me one.

When Michael Richards, the comic, used the word at the Laugh Factory back in 2006, I didn't like it, but it rolled off me like water off a duck's back. I understood and even applauded all of the controversy and outrage over what happened. But I believe that you choose your battles. And this wouldn't be one of mine. I am more concerned about what I think about me than what some comic thinks.

When I step into the recording studio during one of Kanye's sets and hear "nigga" used repeatedly, when I hear my ninety-year-old aunt say it, when I hear it in song lyrics or in the vernacular of so many black people, or when I hear ignorant racists using it supposedly to insult a black person, it garners from me no energy—no willingness to repel the word. I prefer to repel the actual injustice in the world, and I leave the so-called N-word battle to those who still feel like I used to.

What bothers me is not the word "nigger" but the joblessness, the poor housing, the inferior schooling, and the low salaries for all who white racists might label "nigger." For me, hating the word and insisting that it not be used in any context does little if we don't address the underlying issues.

I have come to feel that what is damaging to our psychological health is not being called a nigger, but being treated with disrespect and disdain and being denied privileges and inalienable rights. Take away the word "nigger" and leave all the other atrocities in place and everything remains the same.

Now I know that words are important and that they shape the way people think. But I also know that a word has no power except the power we give it. Blacks don't have to forever hold on to denotations or connotations of the word "nigga" given to us by white people. We have the power to define that word for ourselves and many of our young people have exercised that power.

At this point in my life, it's not so much about racist white people as it is about conscious black people. And for our young people to not only tolerate the word, but also use and embrace "nigga" does not in and of itself indicate a lack of conscious-ness. To me, to be conscious means knowing your power, your strength—even as it has to do with overthrowing the racist notions associated with the so-called N word. Some blacks (and whites, too) don't think that is possible, feasible, or ad-visable. I respect that position. It's just not mine anymore. Holding steadfast to that position (although it may be fine for others to), would signal a lack of consciousness on my part. Why? Because I believe that we can evolve from the defini-tions assigned to words to ourselves.

I may never say anything like, "What's up, my nig?" or even "Nigga, please!" But I don't believe that it's true that those who do say it are necessarily unconscious and unaware of the historical use of the word. In fact, I have known peo-ple who are fully conscious, warriors even, who use "nigga" freely. Whether those in my generation ever embrace the word or not, ever stop pretending that they never use it, ever stop giving the power to it that I used to give to it, is their choice—just like not being mad at the word or the blacks who use it, is my choice.

Another reason I am no longer bothered by the word "nigga" is that I don't feel the use of it is what robs black people of self-esteem. The little black children who indicated a strong preference for white dolls in Dr. Clark's 1950s doll test and again when the test was repeated in 2007, surely did not suffer from self-hate because they were all called nigger on a regular basis. Maybe they had never been called nigger to their faces at all. It was the attitude behind the meaning of the word that was the culprit. Not the word itself. So admittedly, I am not offended any longer when I hear the word in the context of hip-hop culture and I sometimes even sing along when I hear songs like "Gold Digger."

> I ain't saying she's a gold digger. But she ain't
> messing with no broke nigga.

No doubt my emersion in hip-hop culture is to some degree responsible for my change in attitude when it comes to the word "nigga." But I hold my belief primarily because I strongly feel as I said before that the word, in and of itself, is not the root cause of racism in this country. It is simply a bi-product. The word is not the problem. People using the word with a certain intent, a certain disdain are the problem.

As I head now into my late fifties, I have come full circle regarding a word I could scarcely bring myself to say just a couple of years ago. Where I questioned whether or not a word like "nigger" could ever evolve to a term of endearment, and even felt strongly that it could not, I have witnessed that happening.

"Can a generation actually change the meaning or change the context to create a whole other experience?" I wondered.

For me the answer is yes because I have seen it happen. And in seeing it, I have shifted from a paradigm I thought I would hold steadfast to until death to one that has opened up a whole new way of me thinking about the word. Perhaps some of my colleagues and dearest friends would be all but outraged that I could possibly be questioning whether or not there is a context for the word that makes it palatable. After all, my own father was called "nigger" daily as he worked to make a living to support us. How in the world could I ever have anything but disdain for the word in any context? And yet, if I am honest, I must admit this shift in my thinking. I don't invite anyone to share in it unless they want to. And I have no interest in debating the issue. But for me, it's liberating to no longer be bound by a word. It frees me further to fight the real racism behind the word.

I know firsthand that some of today's rappers, Che Smith aka Rhymefest or Lonnie Rashid Lynn, Jr. aka Common, for example, are fully conscious of who they are and are fully aware emotionally and academically of our history. Rhymefest and I have had deep conversations about black people, our heritage, and our struggles since he and Kanye were teens. He, like Kanye, Common, Mos Def, and some others who use the word "nigga" in their music, are clearly conscious and informed and in no way taking anything away from the culture by using the word in his lyrics.

Semantically and rhetorically no other word would have quite the same bite. Not by far, in fact.

That I don't feel the urge to lecture all of the young people in the studio on the word being offensive and inappropriate lets me know that I have evolved, not regressed. Were I to go back to the slave dungeons in Ghana that I visited in 2002, I would feel no less connected, no less pain than I did before my position on the word "nigger" shifted. It was not what the slaves were called, but how they were treated that continues to upset me. I remain racially and politically conscious, and even feel that perhaps the word "nigger" may ultimately undergo the same metamorphosis as did the word "black." Admittedly, the analogy breaks down after a point.

But when I was growing up in the '50s and was not allowed to use the word "nigger," I was not allowed to use the word "black" either. That was just as bad as saying "nigger."

"You old black thing!" was a phrase that I just might get a whipping for if I dared to say it. To be black back then was a bad thing. It was associated with evil, destruction, the worst of the worst. There was no way that you could be considered beautiful, no matter how "keen" your features, how "good" your hair, how shapely your body, if your skin was black.

But James Brown proclaimed, "Say it loud! I'm black and I'm proud!" and the Black Power Movement came into full bloom and suddenly the word had another kind of power. We proudly referred to ourselves as Black and regard those using terms like "colored" or "Negro" to be all but barbaric. "Black" or "blackie" were words white people used to degrade people of African descent just as they used the word "nigger."

The word "black" evolved. Now we've gone from fighting if we were called black, to fighting if we aren't. Despite the negative associations linked to the word or color, it is still our description of choice. We rarely think about or take exception to the language being racist and the color black being associated with something bad today, even though it still has a negative connotation in many ways. The good guys still wear the white hats, the evil ones wear black. The good horse is the white horse, the bad one is black. The lie that's okay to tell is a little white lie. Black hole, blackmail, blackball are all negative. The angel food cake is white or light, while the devil's food cake is dark. There are other examples of how over the years the word "black" or anything dark has taken on a negative connotation. That, in itself, impacts a nation of people, consciously and subconsciously.

There was a point in our history that many were not only offended by the word "black" but were offended to be black. More than a few cents were made from bleaching creams. The affluent underwent cosmetic surgery to alter not just flat noses and thick lips, but dark skin as well. We didn't want to be black. Pure and simple.

But the word evolved, and so did we—to another understanding and another way of perceiving it. Is it possible that any part of this is analogous to the word "nigga"?

My exposure to hip-hop culture and to those in it who I know are racially conscious, has lead me to raise questions I never imagined I would. It was difficult at first for me to even hear the word "nigga" in Kanye's music. Now, it's no big deal. Now I even sing along.

However black people may ultimately come to feel about the word "nigga," for me one thing is certain: It will never be appropriate for a white person to use the word because of what it has meant historically. I realize that it is a double standard, but it is a necessary and an earned double standard, as far as I'm concerned. It's not one that I seek to justify. Some things are just family business. And for the collective black family, I believe that using the word "nigga" is our prerogative alone.

Should racism everywhere in the world and especially in America disappear so completely that not one trace of the impact of slavery and injustice against blacks can be seen or felt at all, perhaps my stance on this would change. Of course, I, nor any other black person can stop any nonblack person from saying "nigga." I'm not the word police. But in expressing the shift in my position on the word "nigga," I hasten to say that for me, it's a word reserved for blacks only. Sometimes at his concerts when Kanye is singing "Gold Digger," he extends special privilege to the whites in the audience.

"White people, this is your only chance to say the word 'nigga' and get away with it," he says. "Take advantage of it."

It's Kanye's way of saying he too feels that the word "nigga" should only be used by blacks. Some whites do take advantage and sing the song right along with everybody else. Inwardly, I become slightly pissed off. There are many whites, however, who are silent on that word, and I respect and appreciate them for that.

That hip-hop has tried to reclaim the word "nigga" and bring new meaning to it doesn't mean that the word has changed completely and that there are no overtones when the word is used in certain contexts. Nevertheless, it is and always has been part of black culture and not only in negative ways. Just as we now look at ourselves as a people who were enslaved rather than a people who were slaves, there is a distinction to be made between the niggers we were called by whites and the niggas we call ourselves. I'm not arguing for this change. But I see it coming. It's a word. Granted, in some contexts, still a volatile word. But again, words have no meaning in and of themselves. It is people who assign meaning.

Kanye understands the historical context of the word "nigger" and I'm certain that his peers do, too. Perhaps to them the idea is to transcend the feeling that created that word and not the word itself.

17

Heard 'Em Say: "George Bush Doesn't Care About Black People"

I hate the way they portray us in the media. You see a black family, it says, "They're looting." You see a white family, it says, "They're looking for food." And, you know, it's been five days [waiting for federal help] because most of the people are black. And even for me to complain about it, I would be a hypocrite because I've tried to turn away from the TV because it's too hard to watch. I've even been shopping before I've even given a donation, so now I'm calling my business manager right now to see what is the biggest amount I can give and just to imagine if I was down there, and those are my people down there. So anybody out there that wants to do anything that we can to help—with the way America is set up to help the poor, the black people, the less well-off, as slow as possible. I mean, the Red Cross

is doing everything they can. We already realize a lot of
people that could help are at war right now, fighting
another way—and they've given them permission to go
down and shoot us! George Bush doesn't care about
black people.

—KANYE WEST, NBC hurricane-relief telethon,

September 2, 2005

The last line was all that people focused on. It was the shot
heard round the world. I was in New York City at the Dream
Hotel, relaxing. I had been doing some Kanye West business
in New York and I didn't actually watch the telethon. I didn't
hear the statement Kanye made live. But later that day, all
week in fact, I heard it over and over and over again as the
news media had a field day.

My phone rang minutes after Kanye said what he said. It
rang off the hook. The first phone call came from one of my
dearest friends, Bill Johnson. It was ironic that he would be
the first to call because he was my Negro History teacher in
high school. I'd been taught from birth, it seems, to be proud
of who I am, proud to be black. Bill Johnson was one who
confirmed and continued those lessons. His class gave me a
strong sense of myself, my culture, and my history and helped
me shape my views on race and ethnicity.

Where justice is denied, where poverty is enforced,
where ignorance prevails, and where any one class is
made to feel that society is in an organized conspiracy
to oppress, rob, and degrade them, neither persons
nor property will be safe.

—FREDERICK DOUGLASS, 1866

What a fitting passage. How ironic also that Bill had taught it in our Negro History class. Now here he was, the first one to dial my number, minutes after Kanye announced to the nation his feelings about George Bush.

"Did you hear what Kanye just said?" was the first thing out of Bill's mouth.

I told him I had not heard.

"Turn on the TV," he said.

I grabbed the remote control and turned on the television. The news was starting to flood in.

"You better beware," he said. "Get ready for a slew of phone calls."

After he told me exactly what Kanye said, my mind started turning.

Kanye was right, I thought. George Bush doesn't care about black people. Hurricane Katrina exposed that truth. And Kanye simply stated it.

As Bill and I talked, everything started sinking in. I began to realize what an enormous impact those seven words were having on the entire country and I wondered what impact Kanye's saying them might have on him personally and professionally. I didn't let fear set in, though. I couldn't afford to. But it was not just an ordinary morning for me. Not at all. "Had he really said it?" I thought to myself. And then I thought, "What next?" Bill and I hung up the phone and he said he'd be available if I needed him. I guess he knew things would start to sink in and perhaps be a little unsettling.

He was right. Concern deepend. Jahon, my best friend in Chicago, called and began talking about what had happened to the great diva Eartha Kitt for speaking her mind. Ms. Kitt had been a huge star, selling many records, topping the charts, selling out shows. In 1968, President Lyndon Johnson and his wife, Lady Bird, invited her to a celebrity women's luncheon at the White House. The president asked Eartha Kitt to give her views on inner-city youth. I guess he thought that as the only black invited, she would have some insight. Instead of talking about inner-city youth, though, she took the opportunity to talk about the Vietnam War and how devastating it was to poor minorities.

She told the truth. But that truth embarrassed Lyndon Johnson and made him so angry that allegedly, he had Eartha Kitt blacklisted. Apparently, people refused to hire her to perform, afraid of a negative backlash. She was put under a secret federal investigation. Her house was bugged and Secret Service agents followed her. Some say when the FBI failed to find any evidence that Eartha Kitt was a threat to national security, they sicced the CIA on her and put together a dossier defaming her character, saying she was a nymphomaniac.

It seems that Eartha Kitt, someone who I admire and respect, was basically run out of America for speaking her mind and telling the truth. That's the history of this government—defaming and destroying those who have the audacity to challenge it. Fortunately, she came back bigger than ever and is considered an icon today. But some people never come back.

Jahon wasn't afraid for Kanye. Like me, she was just somewhat concerned. She had seen him land on his feet before and felt that at the end of the day, it would be no different this time. He had told the truth and, like we say in my family, "it needed to be said."

The calls continued to come in. They came from people I knew well and from people I hardly knew at all. All of them were positive and supportive, however. Not one person was disappointed that Kanye had made the statement. I did think, however, that some may have likened those seven words to another seven—the last seven uttered by Christ.

My former dean, Rachel Lindsay, called. She knew of Kanye's affinity for speaking his mind from his days at Chicago State. My trusted friend and fellow professor Haki Madhubuti called. He'd known Kanye since he was five years old, studying Swahili at the African-centered school Haki and his wife, Safisha, owned. Both Rachel and Haki were always supportive. Haki and I even talked about getting ready and being prepared for a backlash. By this time, I had started to think more realistically about the possibilities. I became a little more anxious. I think the Eartha Kitt story and the Dixie Chicks experience another friend had reminded me of started to weigh a little more heavily on my mind than they should have. Not because they weren't real live examples of what speaking out can bring. But because my faith is unshakable and I knew Kanye had been used as a vessel for those words to come through. My father always taught us, "If God is for you, who can be against you?" I think about his words a lot, especially when I know Kanye has said something God would have him say.

Haki and I began to talk about the whole situation. He told me not to worry, that what Kanye said was true and a lot of people knew it but were too afraid to say so. He applauded Kanye for stepping out of a comfort zone in a way that none of the other entertainers had. He talked about how conscious Kanye was and how he would be protected. As we spoke he was mentally putting in place the army of supporters we would call on if we needed to. If I knew anything, I knew that neither Kanye nor I would be alone. Haki has always been that kind of friend to me. And I have always loved him for his consciousness and his commitment to the liberation of black people. Even if he had not called, I would still know I could count on his support.

I have many friends like Haki: Bart McSwine, Leroy Bryant, and Saleem Muwakkell. And that doesn't begin to exhaust the list. I know they'd have Kanye's back not because he is my son, but because they are warriors who understand that we must stand up and speak out and act on what we feel is important, or we will perish.

After a number of such calls, I finally got one from Kanye.

"What's up, Mom?" he said.

Of course, only one thing was on my mind.

"Kanye, I heard you said that the president doesn't care about black people," I said.

"Yeah."

"You told the truth," I told him. "I'm proud of you."

We kept talking and he sounded emotional. It was clear to me that he had not planned to say what he said, but he was not sorry he had said it. When I think about it, it would have surprised me if Kanye had not said whatever he was feeling at that telethon. He is not someone you can just hand a script to and expect him to follow it verbatim, unless it expresses how he truly feels. The more important the issue, the more passionate he will be about it. What was more important than what went on that ill-fated day in New Orleans?

Kanye is a thinker and a doer. That's how he's wired. How could he be expected to think any differently than he did that day? And being who he is, it's natural that his thoughts would be followed by the statement he made. I can't imagine him *not* calling it like he sees it. Isn't that what we should all do?

It comes natural to him. His father was that way. Ray was very active in the movement, as was I. So we raised Kanye with a certain sensibility. That sensibility runs through the entire family—that consciousness that comes from knowing who you are and believing you have rights that should not and must not be violated.

I've fought for justice all my life, or at least since almost as far back as I can remember. When I was just six years old, I was arrested for a sit-in at a segregated restaurant in Oklahoma City. I remember crying, my little legs dangling over the seat of that big chair at the police station. I wasn't crying because I'd been arrested, though. I was crying because I wanted to ride to jail in the paddy wagon just like my older brother, Porty, and the other big kids. But I was only six and too young for the paddy wagon. I guess I was also too young to be fingerprinted and put in a cell like my brother and the older kids. But that didn't stop me from wanting to be. We were all members of the NAACP Youth Council. Mrs. Clara Luper, who presided over the youth council, had organized us. We knew we were fighting (nonviolently) with a purpose and we knew what that purpose was. I sat in that big chair and waited for my parents to come for my brother and me. And I wasn't scared, not at all. I was mad.

That was in the mid-1950s. The movement hadn't made national headlines yet. There had not been the Montgomery bus boycott or the March on Washington. Emmett Till's brutalized and deformed remains had not yet appeared in *Jet* magazine. Dr. Martin Luther King Jr. wasn't yet a household name. And the image of fire hoses and dogs had not yet gripped the American psyche. But in my hometown and places like it throughout America, coloreds, as we were called then, were fed up. The movement had begun. And I was part of it. It just had not been televised yet.

I was arrested that day along with more than twenty others. We sat in at a hamburger place called the Split-T Restaurant and violated an injunction forbidding us to do so. So they took us to jail. That place is still standing today. I drove by it recently and wondered, "Why did we ever want to eat there?" It's shabby-looking now. But it wasn't then. It was just off-limits to anyone black as were almost all establishments in Oklahoma City and throughout America at that time.

We kept sitting-in, however. We were not deterred by a trip to jail and within two years, almost every restaurant in that city was integrated because of our efforts.

Integrating restaurants would not be Kanye's struggle. But the racism would be just as apparent in Louisiana in 2005 as it was in 1955. It would manifest itself in people left to die on rooftops. We know. We went to the Astrodome and talked with some of the people who were on the roofs. They told us how they'd been thrown body bags and told to put the bodies of their loved ones in the bags if they did not make it. We saw hundreds of them stretched out on cots, wondering where they'd go once the FEMA money ran out and the cot-filled dome had closed. They listened as the president's mother said that some of them were better off than they had been before Hurricane Katrina hit. And we saw their anguished faces.

Kanye had wanted to go to New Orleans to see the devastation firsthand. He was advised to go to Houston instead because by that time dead bodies were floating around in contaminated waters in New Orleans and supposedly all of the people who'd survived had been evacuated to other areas. He went to Houston. We were a delegation of eight. Ray and I joined Kanye. Senator Rodney Ellis and his assistant Karen Domino had worked it out so that Kanye could learn just what he wanted to know.

"What do the people need most?" Kanye asked. "I can't do as much as I would like to, but I can do something. I want to talk to the victims myself and ask them what they need."

I was touched by Kanye's sincerity and determination to help as much as he could. I was also impressed that he would not allow a single camera to follow us.

"I'm doing this as a regular citizen, not a celebrity," he said.

He didn't want any credit or any publicity for any contribution he might make. He wanted to help quietly.

We checked into our hotel and prepared for the next morning. We'd brought some toiletries and other personal items we'd been told would be useful to those we visited at two different churches in the area. Some of the gifts were not altogether practical—like lipstick and fingernail polish for the ladies, and cologne for the men. But I thought that with all the other gift boxes containing only the basics, perhaps to beautify a little or put on a fragrance might not be all bad. The people loved those gifts as well as the monetary contributions we made. For the children, we brought candy and Halloween masks. Wearing them seemed to be the most fun they'd had since the hurricane hit. Those were "I love you" gifts. We returned two weeks later with more substantive contributions.

Our first full day in Houston, we started at the Astrodome. Before entering, we all joined hands and prayed. We
wanted to be guided to say things and do things that would
be most comforting, most meaningful. Our prayers were answered. And when many of the people saw Kanye, they were
thrilled. They were glad that he had said what he had about
the president and they thanked him for it.

Kanye was prepared to speak to the two thousand people
there over the PA system. We'd been told that he'd be able to
and we looked forward to it. That way, he could say something that would be inspiring, hopefully, to all there. As
Kanye started toward the mic to greet the people, however,
he was told that he could not. The Red Cross was in charge
and I guess they'd heard enough of Kanye for a while. It was
too bad. I know it would have lifted the spirits of so many to
know that Kanye was there and that he really cared.

We visited the two churches on the itinerary that day
and Kanye was able to really talk to the people and ask indi-
viduals what they needed. Most responded that they needed
jobs and a place to stay. Partnering with the Urban League to
interview families who'd been displaced, Kanye, through his
foundation, was able to help. Thanks to his generosity, fifteen
families were given a furnished place to stay for one year. It
was to be a transition year, a year to rebuild as much as possible.

When Kanye said those words about the president, he
spoke from his heart that day, and a nation of people heard
him. He was talking about what was happening in New Orleans, but his words transcended that city and the president.
The devastation, as tremendous as it was, is not nearly so tremendous as the poverty, ignorance, and hopelessness that

characterize so many in this country. The attack, if you'd call it that, was not on the man George Bush, but on the government that he heads.

"I have never met George Bush," Kanye told me. "Maybe one-on-one, he's a cool dude."

But what's not cool is the overwhelming despair still rampant in this country. Were that not the case, there would have been far fewer people to side with Kanye. People were even printing T-shirts with Kanye's words on them. The shirts sold out fast. Why? Because people wanted to echo the sentiments of Kanye West. They felt if George Bush cared about black people, the dropout rate among black males in this country would not be fifty-eight percent. Thirty-three percent of black males between the ages of twenty and twenty-nine would not be incarcerated or under some correctional supervision. Unemployment for blacks would not be double that of whites in this country. Seventy-plus percent of black babies would not be born out of wedlock or in orphanages. Almost thirty percent of all blacks would not be living at or under the poverty level. And the list goes on and on and on. Does this seem to you like a country whose leader cares about black people?

George Bush himself said that perhaps he needed to do a better job showing that he cares about black people. How can you claim that you care about something if you don't show it? You can say you care about your children, but if you don't provide for them, do you really care about them? You can say you care about your neighbor, but if you never even speak except in passing or when you want something, do you really care about them? You can say you care about your spouse, but if you beat him or her day and night, do you really care? The proof is in the doing. All the rest is just window dressing, just tinsel on a tree.

In the midst of the craziness around Kanye making that statement, a strange calm came over me, the calm that comes after the storm, the calm that comes in knowing that truth is liberating.

Kanye told a simple truth—one that Stevie Wonder could see. And it was news for weeks around the nation and the world. If the statement were not true, why all the fervor? It's like somebody calling your mama a ho. If she's not a ho, you know she's not and you don't even play into it. But if she is one, you want to fight.

Fight I will. But one thing I don't want to do is fear. We do too much of that as black mothers. We're afraid for our children, especially our male children. That has been part of our legacy. We've taught our children to look down for so long, I'm not sure we know how to teach them to look up. We don't want them to expect too much because we fear they'll be disappointed if they don't get it. I couldn't do that to my child and expect him to grow from a boy to a man. When fear would dare raise its ugly head, I'd just push it back down, or shake it off and keep moving. There was no time for looking down or for tiptoeing around the truth. Not then and not now. We must teach our children to speak their minds and speak the truth with confidence and strength.

Kanye stood strong when those words came through him. And today, he has not been the worse off for it. It actually expanded his popularity enormously. And my respect for him, already as high as I thought it could get, shot through the roof.

So many people came to rally behind him, which was undoubtedly confirming and comforting. Even an ex-boyfriend of mine called to tell me he was not going to drink Pepsi. Pepsi was one of Kanye's endorsements at the time and the rumor was that Pepsi was going to pull their endorsement deal. People everywhere started boycotting Pepsi. We got e-mail and letters in support of Kanye over what they heard. We returned those e-mail messages and phone calls when we could. Thankfully, Pepsi never pulled out of the deal or even thought about it. We wanted all our caring supporters to know that. Instead of ending the relationship, Pepsi actually beefed up play of Kanye's commercial on stations throughout the country, particularly on MTV and BET. Any wonder why they chose those stations?

People who didn't know who he was suddenly wanted to shake Kanye's hand and say thank you. Letters and calls came from people saying, "We got your back!" From Al Branch, who's on Kanye's marketing team, to Al Gore, the former vice president of the United States, Kanye was approached and supported for his so-called brave statement. I don't deny that it was a brave thing to do. But it was also the only thing to do. Like Gitlow says in Ossie Davis's *Purlie Victorious*, one of my favorite plays, "Somebody's got to take a stand for the everlasting glory of our people. Make civil rights from civil wrongs and bring this old nation to a fair and just conclusion."

Kanye took that stand at the telethon by simply telling the truth.

While the truth can set you free, apparently it can also make you act crazy. Would you believe that on the flip side of the coin, some people who had donated to the Red Cross reportedly called and said they wanted their money back? If, in fact, that was the case, it saddens and disappoints me greatly. That people would withdraw their support for human beings and pull back contributions made to lessen human suffering based on something someone said off script at a live telethon, something neither sanctioned nor supported by the Red Cross, is mind-boggling to me. What else can one think but that they, too, didn't care about black people, about poor people, about people in utter despair?

After the fact, Kanye went on a couple of talk shows and was asked about his now infamous comment. On *The Ellen DeGeneres Show*, Kanye shared his feelings about the possibility of losing existing or potential endorsements. He stated forthrightly, "I might lose my endorsements for what I said, but what about the people who lost their families? What about the people who lost their lives?"

That's who he was speaking for that day—the people. They were the source of his pain. Seeing those bodies floating in the water; seeing the abandonment; seeing the lack of food, lack of water, and all too little help; reading about people being shot; seeing how blacks were portrayed as criminals—it was too much.

Heard 'em say; "George Bush doesn't care about black people." Heard him tell the truth.

18

Touch the Sky

Y'all might as well get the music ready 'cause this is going to take a while. When I had my accident, I found out at that moment, nothing in life is promised except death. If you have the opportunity to play this game called life, you have to appreciate every moment. A lot of people don't appreciate their moment until it's passed.

And then you got to tell those Al Bundy stories: "You remember when I..." Right now, it's my time, and my moment. Thanks to the fans, thanks to the accident, thanks to God, thanks to Roc-A-Fella, Jay-Z, Dame Dash, G, my mother, Rhymefest, everyone that's helped me.

And I plan to celebrate, and scream and pop champagne every chance I get, 'cause I'm at the Grammys, baby! I know everybody asked me the question, they wanted to know, "What, Kan, I know he's going to wild out. I know he's going to do something crazy."

Everybody wanted to know what I would do if I didn't win...I guess we'll never know!

—KANYE WEST, Grammy acceptance speech, 2006

That speech was about the whole idea of seizing the moment. To live in the now. To not look back and say, "I shoulda
coulda woulda." This is something that I am learning from
Kanye. I haven't mastered this yet. But I certainly see the need
for carpe diem, to seize the day and really live.

Kanye was saying, "It's my time right now and I'm going
to live it right now!"

When he was on *The Oprah Winfrey Show*, he said that if
we are living life in living color, then he wanted to live it in
bright red—bold, loud, and alive. And I get that. Why be
here on this earth if nobody notices? Why be here if you're
not going to make a difference? Why be alive if you're not
going to live?

We teach best what we most need to learn. We often-
times know something, but we don't live it.

I see things in him that I may have given lip service to, but
he applies them. Relaxing, going into my living room every
day and looking at either the sunrise or the sunset. That's
what I'm doing.

I will not let a day go by that I don't take fifteen to thirty
minutes minutes to smell the roses.

I never did that before. We lived on Lake Michigan for
eight years. Kanye and I and the dog would go out and play
fetch. I would look at the lake, but I never looked all the way
across. You could see the skyline of Chicago, but I would stop
my vision. Kanye never stopped his vision—he took in the
whole picture.

My parents taught me to think about flying, but Kanye is
teaching me to actually fly. I'm a copycat when it comes to
Kanye. I see my whole style changing. I've gone from being a
collector to being a minimalist. I used to want every spot on

the wall covered and I would have so much furniture that I would almost break my leg trying to get through a room Now, my house is sparsely furnished and the art is sparingly and strategically placed.

I realized that I like it that way. It makes me feel less cluttered, freer. I've always lived in homes that were Victorian or Colonial. Now I have an open floor plan with a view of the ocean (Thank you, Kanye, for this birthday present!). And I notice that my demeanor changes in this environment. I have even started doing a little yoga.

The older you get, the more you realize how short life is. Everyone should make a commitment to enjoy every day on this earth, to stop and smell the roses and to make a real attempt to touch the sky!

19

Giving Back:
Loop Dreams

Won't You Please Join Us In Making A Difference . . .
A message from Kanye:
For as long as I can remember, I have dreamed of making a
substantial impact on the music world. Hard work and other
values such as commitment, respect, discipline, integrity, and
responsibility conspired to drive me toward my dream.

Over the past few years, I have had the opportunity to meet
hundreds of young people across this land, and contrary to popular
belief, they also have goals and dreams.

Consequently, I have concluded that prospering in the
world of music is only a piece of what I really want to
accomplish. So I was encouraged—in fact, driven—to
found and develop Loop Dreams, the first initiative of
the Kanye West Foundation. This rap writing and
music production program is designed to involve
students in learning through a hands-on curriculum
we believe will motivate and compel them to stay in
school and graduate.

Loop Dreams is an unprecedented approach to engaging
students in not only the study of hip-hop and the way it can be
used to better our world, but in the development of habits of mind
that are critical to student success no matter what path they
ultimately choose to follow.

I fervently believe that, as someone has said before, "When
you change the way you look at things, the things you look at
change." I want to help change the way young people look at school
and, hence, the way they look at their futures.

Not long after Kanye signed his record deal with Roc-A-
Fella, and before the release of *College Dropout*, he asked me one
of the most important questions he has ever asked: "Mom,
when am I going to start giving back?"

It blew me away. We had talked about a number of things
that day, including whether he'd stay in New Jersey and rent
for a little longer, or whether he would buy something in
Manhattan. I was never big on renting. I'm into ownership
and I was focused on how Kanye would make the break from
the Hudson Tea Building in Hoboken, New Jersey to at least a
one-bedroom condo in the city. But Kanye wasn't very interested in searching for property. His mind was on giving back.

Kanye never got high marks in the "plays well with others" section on his report card. He was an only child and he
never really had to share his toys. Everything he had was his.
I never put him in the Boys Scouts, as my friends had recommended, thinking it would give him a more communal sense.
And he never wanted a little brother or sister growing up,
and told me as much. He was pretty single-mindedly focused
his entire childhood.

So while I wasn't surprised when he asked me that question about giving back, it was not expected at that time. In the first throes of success instead of thinking only about all of the things he would do for himself, he was also thinking about what he must do for others. That was a proud moment for me.

"Well, Kanye," I said. "You can start giving back at any time."

But since there was still not a whole lot of money coming in at the time, I wondered what Kanye had in mind. Paying the rent, which was now substantial, and all of the bills, and buying those extras that he wanted—like the huge pool table and the flat screen TV, the Mercedes-Benz and the designer clothes—wouldn't leave much for charity.

But Kanye had a plan. He decided that he'd give ten percent of whatever he netted to someone less fortunate. He'd just pick somebody, give them the cash, and that would be that. Immediately, I thought that he'd probably had a conversation with his dad about tithing. It made me feel good that Kanye was so intent on giving that he would sacrifice something he could have purchased for himself. But there had to be a better way than just giving cash to someone at random.

"Kanye, it's great that you want to give back," I told him. "Let's look into the best ways to do that very soon."

Kanye is the kind of person that if he has something on his mind, there's no waiting; there's no "very soon." There's only right now. There would be no "looking into it" as far as Kanye was concerned. There would just be doing it. I knew that I had better come up with my own plan if I didn't want Kanye just handing out money.

I'd always thought that Kanye would one day have a foundation. I was confident that he would be rich and famous.

So I came up with an idea to for a 501(C)(3), through which we could raise money to help others. Not only would Kanye be helping others, he'd get a tax break for doing it. All the money he put into the foundation would be tax deductible. It made much more sense than unstructured giving. I shared the idea with Kanye and he got right on board. "Okay, let's do it!" he said.

It was time to go to work. I didn't know much about foundations. I'd never been a part of one. I just knew that lots of people had them and they were doing wonderful things through them. The first person who came to mind was Oprah. Everyone who knows me knows I'm an Oprah fanatic. I've admired her for many years and love everything about her. No way could anyone ever say anything negative about her around me. I wasn't having it. All of my friends know I won't stand for any Oprah bashing. Anyone who'd ever try it would hear it from me. I just can't understand how people who do nothing for anyone but themselves and maybe their families, could say anything negative about someone who does so much for so many.

When I thought about this foundation, Oprah was the first person that I thought of. I went online to read about her foundation to see if there was anything I could garner that might be helpful to us. I thought of the things she'd do to make a difference on her show—little things that were actually huge, like focusing on gratitude and random acts of kindness. The wheels started turning, but I still didn't know what to suggest to Kanye, at least not programmatically.

We decided to launch the foundation without a signature program. It would just be a foundation through which Kanye could give to other foundations or worthy causes. Soon however, Kanye came up with another plan. He decided he wanted to have his own program. Rather than raise money for other worthy causes, he would raise money for a specific purpose and a specific program of his own. He wanted a music production program where he could put music studios in the schools and help motivate students to stay in school and graduate.

He told me that when he was in high school, all he liked was art, music, recess, and lunch. He had grown tired or bored with all the other subjects. Of course, there was no threat of him ever dropping out of high school because he knew I would have killed him first. But still, he struggled through the "academic" courses with no motivation like what he wanted to provide.

"In school, I could never make music I heard on the radio," he said. "If kids have opportunities to do that, maybe they will stay in school."

We talked about the tremendous dropout problem in schools across the nation. And when he learned that more than 50 percent of African American and Latino students drop out of school before graduation, that was it. He knew how he wanted to give back. His would be a drop-out prevention program involving music production and rap. He felt that would definitely motivate kids to stay in school.

Just as kids have "hoop dreams" and want to stay in school to play basketball, Kanye felt that many kids today want to rap and produce music.

"They have loop dreams," he said. And we had our name: Loop Dreams.

It was confirmed when we met Miki Woodard, the then-director of programs at Creative Artist Agency. Miki was very familiar with foundations. In her capacity at CAA, she worked with them all the time. When she heard about the idea, she was instantly on board. Beverly Williams retired early from a thirty-year career in education to come aboard as program director. She knew kids inside out. We were ready to plan and then implement.

Loop Dreams launched at the Accelerated School in South Central, Los Angeles as a one-semester pilot program in the fall of 2006. Seventy-five eighth graders went to their Loop Dreams class everyday where they studied, in an academic setting, the whole of hip-hop culture. They studied the history of rap, famous rappers, the impact of positive vs. negative lyrics, how to create a loop, how to create a track, and careers in the music industry. Each day, students ran to class, excited about making music of their own. They also learned the habits of mind that characterize the program: commitment, respect, discipline, integrity, and responsibility.

Loop Dreams was a big hit.

But it's not always easy to make decisions about such an important project. One night, as I lay thinking about some critical decisions that had to be made, my phone rang. It was Chuck Ortner, the president of the foundation.

He wanted to talk about expanding the Loop Dreams program and suggested that we consider Y's, boys' and girls' clubs and other such venues for program expansion.

Since the foundation was launched in the fall of 2003, Kanye has contributed over four-hundred-and-fifty-thousand dollars to the Kanye West Foundation in support of programs and initiatives designed to help others. And he is seeing his idea come to fruition—and believes that student performance is linked to student passion. When students are passionate about what they are doing, learning becomes fun and they are more likely to achieve the program goals as well as personal goals they set for themselves. Loop Dreams is a rigorous program where students not only learn to write and produce music, they must also demonstrate increased literacy skills, heightened self-worth, and hopefully start the road to self-actualization through the arts.

To Kanye, superstar status carries with it responsibility. It mandates giving back to the world community in proportion to what he has received. His vision, and therefore the vision of the Kanye West Foundation, is not without challenges, but understanding the critical role of education, literacy, and preparedness in the success or failure of young people reaffirms the importance of programs like Loop Dreams.

Kanye and the foundation board members envision the day when the high school dropout rate in cities across the nation will be virtually nonexistent.

It is a well-known fact that kids who drop out of high school often end up in dead-end jobs, unemployed, on the streets, on welfare, in jail, or even dead. The meaningful contributions they could potentially make to themselves, their families, and to the world are lost. Kanye is driven, with the help of the foundation, to put a huge dent in the dropout rate and eventually help eliminate the dropout problem altogether.

Kanye's giving did not begin with Loop Dreams and it doesn't end there. He has made substantial contributions to victims of the Katrina Disaster, and through the foundation, donated money to support Tiffany Person's "Shine On Sierra Leone" project.

Fully committed to alleviating the awful suffering of children in the Sierra Leone mining schools, Tiffany called one day to talk about the grave problems there and inquire about the possibility of Kanye making a contribution. I had never spoken to Tiffany prior to that day, but it was apparent in her voice that not only was the problem dire (a fact well known by all who dare to delve beyond news reports, in which the full story is never told), but that she personally felt driven to help, to do whatever she could to make a difference. After speaking with her, I knew Kanye would not hesitate to make a contribution. Immediately, I hung up the phone and called Kanye to relate to him the discussion I'd just had with Tiffany. He was actually across the world on tour. We spoke for just a couple of minutes. It would not take long for Kanye to be fully onboard. We had not yet established the formal board for the foundation so it would be up to a handful of us to make the decision. It was a no-brainer and I was happy to get back to Tiffany with our affirmative reply.

According to Tiffany, "Through a generous donation from the Kanye West Foundation, 'Shine On Sierra Leone' was able to rehabilitate the first school in the impoverished diamond mining community of Bongema. After ten days of laboring from dawn to dusk, the school was reborn with a brand-new roof, cemented floor, painted interior and exterior walls, repaired toilets, and a new iron door with locks."

Tiffany told us she'd be forever grateful for the initial support from the Kanye West Foundation. But we are more grateful to her for her vision, commitment, and hard work. Through her efforts, the Sierra Leone Foundation was launched and will "be the face for improving the lives of thou-sands of children devastated by poverty, yet living on rich soil."

Thankfully, Kanye has found many ways to give back. Ways as small as talking to a distraught teenager who'd just lost her best friend in a car accident to as large as doing a full concert in New York City to benefit colon cancer research.

"Wake up, Mr. West. Wake up, Mr. West," says the teacher on Kanye's *Late Registration* album. This teacher is in-sistent that Kanye, asleep in class, must wake up and pay attention. I'm here to inform that teacher and everyone else that Mr. West is awake. He's not only awake, but he's also aware—aware that giving back is not only an obligation, but a privilege.

EPILOGUE

I've heard it said more than once that Kanye's success came overnight. People felt that because he rose from virtual obscurity to superstardom in what they believe to be a relatively short period of time, he must have snapped his fingers and all of a sudden became the Kanye West we know today. Well, that just isn't so. Kanye has worked long and hard for what he has achieved and he still does. There is nothing magical about his success. It took and still takes persistence, discipline, commitment, and resilience. Those are a few of the qualities I tried to instill in Kanye from the very beginning. I would talk to him even before he was born. Yes, while he was still in my womb. I believe there is value in that. I believe that the stage must be set before the play ever begins.

I am fortunate to have a son like Kanye. And from all indications, he feels fortunate to have a mother like me. I remember like it was yesterday feeling down sometimes about one thing or another. It may have been because I had more bills than money at the time. It may have been because of some romantic breakup. It may have been that biorhythms were just not in sync that day. But all I needed to do was look down at those smiling eyes Kanye always had, and the sadness would just roll away. It worked every time.

I have talked to other mothers who have experienced the same thing. Even now, when my friend and colleague, Jeanella Blair and I speak about her five-year-old son, Julian, or when I watch video clips on her BlackBerry of him singing "You Are My Sunshine," or making up lyrics about how much he loves his mom, I know all over again why it was imperative that I give birth to and raise at least one child. Nothing is more fulfilling, at least not to me.

When Susan Linns, my confidant and many times my right hand, and I speak about her very heart and soul, six-year-old Dareious, I am reminded of how I felt when Kanye was an infant, a toddler, and a preschooler. And I am gratified all over again. Sometimes I play the voice-mail messages Dareious has left, thanking me for the least little gift I have sent to him, and I can't help but think of Kanye at age six. I reflect on how I knew then he was quite special. Somehow, I knew that he'd have a gift to share with the world. And I knew I had to cultivate that and nurture him so that he could do the work he was sent here to do.

I am grateful that even with all the mistakes I surely made in raising Kanye, I was able to impart some wisdom, some knowledge that has apparently stuck with him all these years.

I've heard Kanye say that the one thing he appreciates

about how he was raised was being able to question anything without being shut down. It is important that kids are not only seen, but heard. I have never believed it should be any other way. Of course, kids have their place, and they should understand and respect that. But that place must be broad and safe. It must be a place where there is room to make mistakes and to learn from them.

I had to learn that children have to have room to roam and at the same time have boundaries so that that roaming does not become detrimental. I had to learn that unconditional loving does not mean unconditional giving. Instead, it means never ever turning your back on your child no matter what. You must always be there and put their needs in front of your own. That was not difficult for me because much of my life centered around making sure Kanye got the best care I could possibly conceive of giving him. I never felt put out in the least because, quite frankly, his happiness was mine.

Now I had a life and activities that did not always include Kanye. But I never had a day pass that he was not central to—even if I was miles and miles away. The psychological connection can sometimes be stronger than the physical one. And when that is the case, love transcends the miles and creates a feeling of security in a child that makes him know he can do anything if he is encouraged and adequately prepared. Love is fundamental but it is not enough. That love must translate into knowing where your child is at all times, seeing to it that the homework and other chores are completed, going places together and communicating honestly and regularly. Any parent can say, "I love you," but you must show up with that love, not just express it verbally.

I have always been a romantic, not just in the sense of a

significant other, but about life and all it encompasses. So I romanticized what was possible in raising Kanye. For me, everything was. We didn't have a lot of money, but we saw places in the far most corners of the world. We didn't have twenty-four hours a day to spend together, but we established a bond that could not and cannot be broken. We didn't and don't always agree, but we respected and respect each other's right to an opinion.

Sometimes when people see me on the street and recognize that I'm Kanye West's mother, they ask me what I did to raise such a brilliant and respectful child. It surprises me sometimes that what they remember is who he is inside as reflected in his lyrics, not his persona, which may sometimes seem a little too blunt and forward for some. I smile and say thank you when they compliment me, knowing that much of my success as a parent came from being blessed with a bright, inquisitive, mischievous, and creative son. It seems to me that he came straight from the womb like that and my job would be to focus almost single-mindedly on providing a nurturing and intellectually challenging childhood for him. Sometimes I had to say no, when I really wanted to say yes. Sometimes I had to sacrifice what I may have preferred doing at the moment to see to it that he did what he was supposed to do.

The aim of parenting is the overall development of the child. Anything that might impact that in any negative way should be avoided at all costs. From an early age, children must be taught integrity and the best way to teach it is to demonstrate it. They must be taught success and the best way to teach success is to be successful by your own standards.

I was lucky. Even before Kanye was born I had achieved

some things that would contribute to my success as a person first, and then as a parent. I knew who I was fundamentally and this is critical. I had a couple of degrees by the time Kanye was born but my father, who valued education as much, if not more, than anyone I have ever known, taught me that all the degrees in the world would be worthless if you can't get along with people. I was also taught to put God first and that has never failed me. I believe, above all else, that my unshakable faith in God brought about all I needed to provide for my child monetarily, emotionally, intellectually, and spiritually.

I am convinced you cannot be a good parent if you are not a good person. And to be the best parent, you must strive to do your best every day. When you do your best every day, then you can insist that your child do the same. Having high expectations is also critical. If you don't expect your child to go far and wide—and no teacher, preacher, or some responsible adult steps in with those expectations—it is unlikely that your child will reach for the moon or the stars. And you may rob them of their greatness.

It's been said that there are no manuals that come with children when they arrive on this earth. You're not sent home from the hospital with a list of definitive actions that will result without fail in your child becoming a well adjusted, fulfilled, actualized, happy adult. Not even Dr. Spock could offer the magic formula. But having raised Kanye, I'm not so sure those formulas don't exist. The problem is they are so all encompassing and so specific to each child they defy being put on paper. But for certain, every child needs parents who are absolutely devoted to their well being at every turn. Caring does not necessarily mean coddling any more than teaching means merely telling. The responsibility of the parent is to figure out just what is appropriate and effective, and supply whatever that is consistently.

The greatest joy I have ever experienced is the joy of raising Kanye. If anything at all tops that, it's how the investment turned out and the love I receive from him for putting in the time when he was coming up. I was nearly twenty-eight years old when Kanye was born, and that worked well for me. It gave me time to complete most of my formal education and to learn some valuable lessons that I had not learned at eighteen. Lots of people become parents much younger than that and they do just fine. They raise fabulous children who turn out well and make invaluable contributions to the world. But whether a child is conceived at sixteen or forty-six, his best shot at success is growing up in a loving and nurturing household with parents or a parent or guardian who insists on excellence and rewards it as well.

I never thought when Kayne was born I would ever write a book about raising him. What I thought about was trying to be the best mother there ever was. Since Kanye is an only child, I had no prior experience at being a parent. But I knew full well that love, faith, patience, exposure, high expectations, good communication, and trust were a few of the things I valued most and that they would be fundamental in raising a boy to manhood. I'm as grateful for having had Kanye as I am for life itself.

And I'm grateful, too, for this opportunity to share my story.